RUNNYMEDE RESEARCH

Education for Some

A summary of the Eggleston
Report on the educational
and vocational experiences
of young black people

The Runnymede Trust

Published by the Runnymede Trust 1986
178 North Gower Street, London NW1 2NB
ISBN 0 902397 63 X

Designed by Hilary Arnott
Typeset by Nancy White
Printed by Trojan Printing Co-operative

Preface

This pamphlet provides a summary of the report, *Education for Some: the educational and vocational experiences of 15-18 year old young people of minority ethnic groups*, also known as the 'Eggleston Report' after the director of the research, John Eggleston, Professor of Education at the University of Warwick.

The report was based on a three and a half year research project, funded by the Department of Education and Science, intended to provide information on the relationship between ethnic minority group membership and educational and vocational experiences. The research looked at the attitudes and aspirations of black pupils; teachers' attitudes and their effect on black pupils' achievement; factors affecting the pupils' choice of school subjects; allocation to ability 'bands'; remedial groups; suspensions; enrolment for examinations; examination results; experiences of further education and the careers service. The research also looked in detail at young black people's experiences of the labour market and the Youth Opportunities Programme.

Perhaps the most important feature of the report is that it candidly examines racist attitudes among teachers and provides clear, substantiated evidence of their presence. The leader column of *The Times Educational Supplement* stated:

> By dint of keeping a low profile, and after much patient negotiation with the minority organisations, the team has produced the report we have long needed — moderate in tone, going straight to the facts, and leading to some provocative conclusions. It demonstrates beyond a peradventure that racist attitudes and practices are currently doing much to hinder the education of Afro-Caribbean pupils. It also shows that many of those pupils are coming to see academic qualifications as an essential defence against the discrimination they fear they will meet in the labour market. It identifies the point at which the problem intensifies — the third year of secondary school — and it lays bare the cycle which often begins, with prejudice on the part of the teachers becoming a self-fulfilling prophecy, so that black pupils lose interest in work and accordingly get themselves assigned to the lowest streams.

In so doing the project was able to go considerably beyond both the evidence and conclusions of the Swann Report and has finally made it possible to talk clearly and constructively about the problems of teacher racism in Britain.

Although the report received little publicity when presented to the Department of Education and Science at the end of February 1985, it achieved widespread attention when it eventually became available to the press in October of that year. The Runnymede Trust, in collaboration with Professor Eggleston, has decided to produce this summary in order to make the report's important findings more widely available.

For the sake of brevity we have had to exclude most of the illuminating quotations and interviews from teachers, careers officers and the pupils themselves which are used extensively in the report. The whole of Chapter Seven of the original report, which discusses case studies of individual black pupils, has been excluded from this summary, as have the appendices which cover further interviews with black pupils, statements by careers officers, a paper by Peter Skinner and Jane Moon entitled *The school leaving experiences of boys from a London comprehensive school*, and the questionnaires used in the survey. We have also excluded Chapter Two of the original report, which reviews the major issues raised by previous research. Our summary, therefore, concentrates on the statistical findings of the survey, and the conclusions and recommendations of the research team. We strongly recommend people to read the full report* in order to share the wider insight which the discursive evidence gave the researchers, and which made an important contribution to their disturbing findings.

As far as has been possible, this summary uses the language of the report itself and includes no editorial comment. The choice of what to include (and what to leave out), and of emphasis, is that of the publishers, although Professor Eggleston has approved the pamphlet as being a fair and accurate summary of his report.

---

* The full report has now been published in book form, entitled *Education for Some*, by John Eggleston, David Dunn and Madhu Anjali, available from Trentham Books Limited, 30 Wenger Crescent, Trentham, Stoke-on-Trent ST4 8LE. Price £12.95. ISBN 0 948080 06 X.

Contents

	Introduction	1
1.	The project	3
2.	The young people	5
3.	Future aspirations	7
4.	The background to choice at 16	10
5.	School processes: an ethnographic study	13
6.	The careers service	26
7.	Destinations and examinations at 16+	35
8.	Young people in continuing education	40
9.	Young people in the labour market	45
10.	Schemes for unemployed school leavers	48
11.	Conclusions and recommendations	51

Introduction

This document reports a three and a half year research project undertaken at the University of Keele. The research was directed by Professor John Eggleston; the researchers were Madhu Anjali, David Dunn and Terry Leander.

The aims of the research as expressed in the project proposal were:

> to provide an enhancement of our knowledge of the link between education provision and ethnic group membership, aspirations, achievement, and employment... Areas of special opportunity and disadvantage and the ways in which these were related to distinctive occupational and social characteristics would be illuminated... Most fundamentally it is to be hoped that the project would illuminate the major unevennesses between supply and demand of labour and educational opportunity which so disadvantage many minority groups and provide information that could allow the development of policies leading to a more effective matching between opportunity and need than exists at present.

This study has, therefore, enabled us to present information on the relationship between ethnic minority group membership and educational and vocational experiences. It should be stressed though, at the outset, that since 1979 the employment situation for almost all young people in Britain has altered considerably. Between October 1979 and October 1982, when our students might have been able to look for work, unemployment for under-18-year-old school leavers more than doubled. Registered youth unemployment rose from 11.4% to 24.6%, excluding participants on special programmes.

Increases in unemployment always have disproportionately severe effects on black people in Britain. Furthermore, young black people face severe difficulties in obtaining work in all circumstances. The cumulative effects of labour market forces and racial discrimination in employment provide an inescapable background for this study, fundamentally affecting both its data and the conclusions to which they lead.

Firstly, very few of our black school leavers have informed us that they have successfully found work. This limits the conclusions we may draw on the relationship between job outcomes and educational characteristics. Secondly, the changing labour market circumstances appear to have reinforced in our students the existing tendency for black young people to persevere in continuing education. For this reason relatively few members of our sample took advantage of the special schemes open to 16-year-olds in 1982-3.

The conjunction of national trends augmented by local difficulties led to especially severe effects in some of the research localities. In one area only one boy and no girls found work out of a total of 306 statutory age school leavers of Afro-Caribbean origin. Young people of Asian background fared little better. At times it appeared that an essential element of our study — jobs — seemed to be disappearing entirely; there seemed little information that even a sophisticated examination of existing services could offer to ameliorate the operation of wider and stronger economic forces. In such circumstances it is tempting to agree with blanket prescriptions such as 'The main problem remains one of racism and discrimination, not the poor educational performance of black kids'. However, we shall show this to be an inadequate condensation of the current complexities of the transition from school to work. The following chapters review our evidence on this complex and shifting area and present our attempts to analyse the vein of fact and opinion we have tapped.

1. The project

The responses to the problems of education for life in a multi-cultural society and opportunities for youth employment are among our most central contemporary concerns; they converge in the educational and occupational experiences of young members of ethnic minorities. There is no shortage of discussion of these issues and, in the face of an apparent plethora of research, it may well be asked — 'why more?'. Yet all existing and prospective research offers little information on the relationship between ethnic minority membership, aspirations, qualifications and other achievement and employment, and the characteristics of courses and institutions.

These unexplored areas give rise to many questions of considerable importance. They include: how successful (relatively and absolutely) are young people of minority ethnic groups in obtaining the various examination qualifications available in schools? Do their successes in these examinations have the same consequences for occupational choice as those of majority group children (ie, can they overcome discrimination)? How do their successes stem from their previous school experience? What of their opportunity for access to continuing further and higher education? How effective is their use of such opportunities between 16 and 18 and what are the consequences of such opportunities? Is there any evidence that the overriding influence derives from socio-economic status rather than ethnicity?

When employment opportunities for all young people are restricted and opportunity for continuing education likely to become more restrictive, there is an urgent need to attempt to answer these and similar questions as a basis for formulating policy and practice. Existing educational research, like that on employment and attitudes, offers approaches rather than answers.

Research design

The core of the project was the study of a group of young people who reached the statutory school leaving age in the school year 1981-82. This group was selected from 23 comprehensive schools in six local authorities. In each school one mixed ability tutor group was chosen for study.

The experiences of the cohort were studied by various means. The young people themselves were given formal and informal interviews, and completed questionnaires. Adults closely associated with their progress were also selectively interviewed on topics of concern to the project.

We also undertook a study of contextual data on young people and statutory provision within the six local authorities, as well as an intensive ethnographic and statistical survey of two schools in a seventh local authority. The synthesis of data acquired by a variety of research techniques at different stages of the young people's progress was integral to the research design.

Schools and localities

The LEAs of Bedfordshire, Birmingham, Bradford, Ealing, Hounslow and ILEA were approached. The three London boroughs were chosen so as to form a transect across the city from inner to outer London, crossing known areas of minority residence. Bedfordshire was selected as a county authority and for the town of Bedford which has a varied minority population. Bradford was chosen to exemplify a textiles town with a substantial proportion of Muslims amongst its minorities, whilst Birmingham was selected as the focus of the region with the second highest black population in England. The selection of individual schools was determined by the wish to have catchment areas with varying economic circumstances and (with two intentional exceptions) with several black pupils in each tutor group; to have schools of varying history and organisation; to have a head teacher likely to cooperate; *not* to have a group of purely 'showplace' schools; and to include single-sex schools.

Notes on terminology

Overall, we use the label 'black' to include all people whose physical characteristics might be likely to lead to their encountering racial discrimination in the British context. For us this category therefore includes people of South Asian ethnic origin.

2. The young people

The cohort

The cohort consists of 562 young people (291 boys and 271 girls). Twenty-eight per cent (157) can be regarded as of South Asian ethnic origin. A further 19.5% (110) can be termed 'Afro-Caribbean', of whom 103 (18.3%) have one or both parents born in the West Indies. The remainder we classify as 'white'.

The Afro-Caribbean cohort: family origins

Among the Afro-Caribbean respondents 55 reported that both their parents were born in Jamaica. Birthplaces were also noted in 11 other Caribbean islands or Guyana, with 22 pupils having both parents born in these localities and a further seven, one parent. Ten pupils noted one or both parents' country of birth simply as the 'West Indies', while others were unknown or not recorded on the questionnaire.

Other research suggested that pupils of Jamaican backgrounds might have lower educational attainments than other West Indian children. We examined several variables relating to examination performance and educational persistence, comparing those of wholly or partly Jamaican parentage with others, and found no significant differences between such groups.

Family background: pupils of South Asian ethnic origin

Information on religious background was deduced from young people's names and interviews with them and teachers. Over 40% of the Asian pupils were found to have a Sikh background, 26.8% were Hindu, 24.2% Muslim and 8.9% other (probably Hindus, but perhaps Sikhs).

The young people were also asked to specify which languages they were able to speak. Multilingualism amongst Asian pupils was found to be frequent; many young people claimed to be able to speak either Urdu and Punjabi or Hindi and Punjabi, and some all three. It is likely that the majority of these have Punjabi backgrounds.

Parents

Questions were asked on the present occupational status of both mothers and fathers. Each produced a pattern of differences which was statistically significant, with black parents more frequently unemployed. Over 25% of Asian pupils said their fathers were unemployed, compared to 20.8% of Afro-Caribbean and 5.7% of white pupils. For mothers, the figures were 8.9% for both Asian and Afro-

Caribbean pupils and 2.8% for white pupils. Asian pupils were also far more likely to regard their mothers as full-time housewives (42.6% of Asians compared to 23.3% of whites and only 10.7% of Afro-Caribbeans).

We also asked for information about either the present or former occupations of parents, and our findings suggest that the fathers of the Afro-Caribbean young people were less likely to be in non-manual occupations than others, but were more likely to be in skilled manual occupations. Further, if at work, the mothers of our young people of Asian origin were more likely to be in semi-skilled or unskilled manual occupations than others. Afro-Caribbean mothers, however, were the most likely to be in professional or intermediate occupations.

Attitudes to school and school work

Homework

Asian pupils in the cohort claim to spend most time doing homework, and are also a little more likely to claim that they do not get enough homework. Pupils of Afro-Caribbean origin are slightly less likely than white pupils to claim that they do under one hour of homework per evening, and are also less likely to claim that they get too much homework than are white pupils.

General attitude measures

Asian pupils in general have a more favourable attitude to school than white pupils, are more likely to be conformist within school, and are more likely to believe that it is important to do well than white pupils within the cohort. Afro-Caribbean pupils were also more likely to believe that it was important to do well in school than were white pupils. There was also evidence of a slight tendency for Asian pupils to express more instrumental and less idealistic and social reasons for attending school; and for the white pupils to have the reverse inclinations.

3. Future aspirations

We begin by looking at the occupations aspired to by fifth year leavers seeking employment in 1982. About one-third of the cohort (34%) believed they would be seeking work immediately on leaving school, though inconsistency in some responses indicates predictably that many were holding their options open. Within this one-third, the proportion of black and white leavers differed greatly from the composition of the full cohort. Nearly half (47%) of the white young people were considering seeking work in 1982, but only one-fifth of the black group (19.9%). It is therefore possible that the two groups of leavers differ in aspects other than race.

The vast majority of Asian, Afro-Caribbean and white boys aspired to skilled manual occupations. No Asian boys and only 4.3% of Afro-Caribbean boys aspired to professional occupations. This compared with 12.5% of white boys. For girls, the majority in all racial groups aspired to non-manual occupations. About 7% of both Asian and white girls aspired to professional occupations, while no Afro-Caribbean girls had these aspirations.

There was no evidence that black leavers were 'over-aspiring' in their choice of job when compared with their white peers. Indeed, for those actually specifying occupations, there was a slight suggestion that some whites might actually hope to get jobs which are 'better' in some way — though the evidence does not support this conclusion. There was also an indication from the proportion of missing responses that black leavers might be slightly less likely to be in a position to choose a job that they 'hope to' start — a suggestion supported by other evidence from both interview and questionnaires, but arising from a number of causes including labour market factors.

The levels of jobs actually achieved illustrated that aspirations and applications were little higher than the job outcomes actually achieved by the successful few. However, six of the 'successful' did have semi-skilled or unskilled jobs, which were unpopular with all leavers — and especially with black young people.

To summarise, there were few evident differences in the levels and types of occupation aspired to and applied to by leavers in each ethnic group, though the low numbers responding demand caution in interpretation. What is most notable about leavers is that a lower proportion of black than white leavers were entering the job market, and those doing so were less likely to have a job arranged before leaving school. Even among the whites, very few had got jobs at a stage when in former years many more would have their immediate future secured.

Future directions

In the fifth year questionnaire the young people were asked when they were most likely to leave school. Despite the 'don't know' responses, certain differences are apparent. Asian pupils were less certain of their scholastic future and less likely to leave at the statutory school leaving age than Afro-Caribbean and white pupils. Both Afro-Caribbean and Asian pupils were more likely to be contemplating a one-year sixth form course than whites, while whites and Asians were more likely to be envisaging a school career involving 'A' level examinations.

This picture of school-leaving intentions is enhanced by the responses to a question asking where the young people were most likely to be in one year's time. Only 15 pupils (2.8%) of the whole cohort believed they would be participating in YOP, and 16 (3%) out of work. As we shall see in later chapters, this expressed optimism was entirely unwarranted. The higher proportions of young Asians and Afro-Caribbeans expecting to remain in education were, however, borne out in later realities.

Pupils hoping to return to school in September 1982 were asked why they intended to enter the sixth form. Many young people in all groups acknowledged that they would be likely to be re-sitting examinations in the sixth form. There are, however, differences between groups; with whites being more likely to stipulate 'A' levels as a reason for staying on at school, and blacks 'O' levels.

Long-term aspirations

In the long term, black respondents had higher aspirations than whites as a group — though there is a notable exception to this generalisation within the groups. Asian boys were most likely to aspire to professional occupations in the long term, while Afro-Caribbean and white boys favoured skilled manual occupations. Both Afro-Caribbean and Asian girls were most likely to aspire to professional occupations (67.7% and 45.8% respectively), while for white girls non-manual occupations were more popular. We have already seen that black young people were envisaging a greater investment in education, both at schools and colleges; and we shall see later that they were also more intent on entering higher education. These occupations were therefore not necessarily aspired to without considerable thought to the time in studying and the qualifications necessary as prerequisites.

In all groups and both sexes the rejection of semi-skilled and unskilled manual occupations was marked, and often coincided with disparaging remarks about their parents' occupations in interviews. There seemed to be a common desire among pupils that they should 'better themselves' in some way. This tendency seems to be particularly noticeable amongst the Afro-Caribbean girls. Lest this be immediately dismissed as 'unrealistic', it should be noted that the mothers of the Afro-Caribbean young people appear to have by far the highest occupational levels of all the mothers in our sample. The occupational aspirations of all black young people must also be viewed in the context of their parents' tendency to be in undesirable jobs in declining manufacturing industry, or to be unemployed.

Given the unattractive occupational position of many of their parents, labouring or operative jobs were unlikely to hold great appeal. The location of many of our young people in Bradford and Birmingham may assist in rendering many skilled occupations similarly unattractive as their insecurity has been evident in recent years.

We found that careers officers seemed to suggest occupations at levels rather close to those chosen by Asians and whites — though it is interesting that the officers' suggested level is lower for the former and higher for the latter groups when compared with young people's own plans. For Afro-Caribbean pupils careers officers suggest lower social class occupations, and teachers do the same for black pupils as a whole. However, the low numbers responding here present grave difficulties, and no firm conclusions can be reached. The theory that professionals are 'cooling out' black pupils by lowering their aspirations — or alternatively helping them by giving 'realistic' advice — cannot be supported from this data alone.

Summary

The evidence of this chapter shows generally realistic patterns of job expectation. Yet there are underlying differences in optimism and pessimism that distinguish black and white young people. For example, many black young people are more optimistic about the advantages of extended education. Yet they tend to envisage continued education in terms of re-taking 'O' levels or CSE examinations and fewer apply for admission to further education. Conversely, white young people envisage taking 'A' levels rather than 'O' levels if they 'stay on' and even apply for entry to colleges of further education. The implementation and consequences of these patterns will be explored in subsequent chapters.

4. The background to choice at 16

School subjects

The cohort was asked to assess the relative importance of themselves, mother, father, teachers and friends when making the choice of school subjects. The majority saw themselves as the most important person involved in subject choice. Parents were seen as less important, though more important than teachers. Black respondents tended to regard teachers as more important than white respondents did. There were also slight differences between groups in the roles played by their respective parents, with Afro-Caribbean and white children regarding their mothers as most important in this decision (50% and 56% respectively compared with 38% of Asians), while Asian pupils reversed this order (50% of Asians felt the father was more important, compared with 29% of Afro-Caribbeans and 42% of whites).

We also asked if there were school subjects that respondents wished to follow but were not able to do so. More than half the cohort were dissatisfied with their schooling on this account. Ethnic differences were slight, though Asians seemed slightly more likely to feel aggrieved.

An interesting manifestation of the 'utilitarian' response to subject choice was that there was no evidence of demand for ethnic languages or any other subjects based on minority cultures. Such subjects appeared to be viewed as less 'marketable'.

When asked about 'favourite' subjects few ethnic differences appeared, except that Asian boys were particularly likely to mention maths and sciences excluding biology, and unlikely to mention English as a favourite subject.

Experiences of work

Part-time or weekend jobs

Significant differences were revealed between ethnic groups in their prior exposure to the world of paid work. Asian pupils were the least likely, and whites the most likely, to have participated in the child labour market (28.8% and 69.7% respectively, compared with 50% of Afro-Caribbeans). Asians were far more likely, however, to have helped out in the family business (42.5% compared with 20.7% of whites and 15.5% of Afro-Caribbeans). When those who hadn't done part-time work were asked their reasons, Asians were more likely not to be allowed to do so, and Afro-Caribbeans not to be able to find any, even though they wanted to do it.

Experiences of visiting employers and employment agencies

Only 10% of all respondents regarded themselves as having visited any local employers with their school. Rather more had visited employers 'on their own or with friends': a total of 16.7% of respondents. Of these, white and Afro-Caribbean young people were more likely to have done so than were Asians.

At Easter 1982 only 3% had ever visited a private employment agency. However, 15.8% had visited a Careers Office and almost a quarter (22.6%) had been to a Jobcentre. Fewer Asians had visited the latter two varieties of agency in proportion to other young people.

Parental contact with schools

There were considerable differences between ethnic groups in reported contacts of mothers and fathers with the school. Mothers of white and Afro-Caribbean pupils were particularly likely to attend schools for parents' evenings and discussing progress in school (84% of both white and Afro-Caribbean mothers had been to parents' meetings). Fathers of white and Asian pupils were next most likely to attend for these purposes. Afro-Caribbean mothers were also reportedly considerably more likely than any other group of parents to go to schools to discuss their children's future job or career (35%). Indeed, given their probable greater likelihood of working full time and perhaps working shiftwork, their diligence when compared with other parents is particularly noteworthy. The rather lower proportion of parents, and especially mothers, of Asian origin attending school to discuss their children was frequently accounted for in interviews by language difficulties. These cannot on any account absolve schools from a responsibility to parents and children. Some teachers suggested that there are schools in which black parents are made to feel less welcome than in others. Any differences between ethnic groups attending school functions must be considered in the light of this suggestion for we have shown that in each group pupils' parents are equally likely to be regarded as interested in their child's future. Stories of schools with similar catchment areas where in some nearly all minority parents attend and in others few are not uncommon. Yet again, we should perhaps seek possible explanations in the institutional structures and arrangements of schools rather than in the characteristics of the individual parents.

Statutory careers advice and information

A large number of pupils claimed never to have spoken on their own to a careers adviser. When pupils were seen by teachers and officers, ethnic minority pupils were slightly less likely to view the advice received as helpful.

Fewer ethnic minority pupils had talked about staying on at school with careers officers than were actually contemplating the course of action. Given the implications for their future, this seems slightly disturbing.

Summary

The influence of parents is generally more significant than that of careers officers and teachers — particularly from Afro-Caribbean mothers and Asian fathers respectively who tend to have greater contact with the schools. And this influence seems closely linked to the overriding subject preferences of the young themselves — to concentrate on achievement in high status, mainstream subjects wherever possible. The young people seem to have little doubt that even modest achievement in 'marketable' subjects is preferable to high achievement in 'non-marketable' subjects. As elsewhere the convergence of street wisdom and conventional wisdom is notable.

5. School processes: an ethnographic study

This chapter is based upon a related study undertaken by Cecile Wright.

Introduction

Throughout this report there are many observations on how schooling may affect the progress and aspiration of ethnic minority pupils. Some of these are tentative rather than definitive: in a study involving 23 schools it is impossible to generate evidence to support all possible hypotheses. Schools are not alike; what may affect pupils adversely or beneficially in one school may not in others. The implementation of policies varies as do policies themselves: both are affected by the differing contexts in which schools exist.

We have made suggestions about attitudes and stereotypes that may be held by teachers and the effect these may have on pupils. We have also suggested that internal structures of schools and their operation sometimes have differential effects on pupils of ethnic groups. To explore such suggestions an SSRC/ERSC 'link student' attached to the project examined two schools in a Midlands authority not otherwise investigated. Acting on her own initiative but with the guidance of the research team, the researcher examined certain aspects of those schools in a manner which generated information of a kind not otherwise accessible to the project — though we have been able to attempt to replicate her evidence in other schools attended by our cohort. *Accordingly it must be emphasised that the chapter only describes events at the two schools under review and is not intended to offer a picture of the state of affairs elsewhere.*

It was agreed that an age-group one year younger than the main sample be studied to facilitate closer examination of the process of placement of pupils into sets and groupings for public examinations. Pupils in the selected year group were examined through classroom observation in two Midlands schools with approximately 900 hours of observation in each school.

Formal and informal interviews were undertaken with individuals and groups of teachers, pupils and other persons associated with the schools. Each school provided access to confidential school records and reports.

Two Midlands schools: a description

Schools A and B are mixed comprehensives approximately three miles apart. The ethnic compositions of the two schools vary considerably. The proportion of pupils of Afro-Caribbean and Asian origin within School A is approximately 25% whereas for School B the ethnic minority pupils comprise over 60% of the school population. Despite this, the school experiences of the Afro-Caribbean pupils in both schools appear to be rather similar.

School A

Although this school has been a mixed comprehensive for the past nine years, there is still a strong grammar school ethos amongst a section of the senior teachers. These teachers exerted considerable influence within the school, because they held positions as heads of departments or as year heads. They saw themselves as wanting to get on with the teaching of their subject but were frustrated by teaching in a comprehensive school rather than a selective school and by what they saw as the poor quality of the pupils. This in turn led to feelings of disillusionment.

School B

School B became a mixed comprehensive in 1972 by amalgamating two single-sex secondary modern schools and a girls grammar school. Some members of staff felt that it had suffered and was still suffering from the effects of the reorganisation.

There is a strong academic ethos amongst some of the senior teachers, though this is sometimes more a sense of nostalgia than something realised in their teaching.

Since the reorganisation the ethnic composition of the school has gradually increased until the proportion of minorities entering the first year is well over half the pupils. This intake of children from ethnic minority groups has sometimes been associated negatively with perceived problems within the school, including perceived declining standards and discipline. A year head who originally came from the secondary modern school at the time of reorganisation argued:

> This school is a low ability school because of its catchment area, which consists of a low social class and a high immigrant population. More fundamentally, it is the high proportion of immigrants in this school which is responsible for the lowering of standards.

This view was held by many members of staff.

For teachers at School A the frustration of having to teach what they considered as 'inferior' pupils is further exacerbated by their perception of having to contend with 'troublesome black pupils'. Similarly some teachers at School B felt dissatisfied with having to teach predominantly 'immigrant' children, with their 'alien' ways, and having to put up with 'disruptive and troublesome Afro-Caribbean pupils'.

Teachers' attitudes

School A

It is difficult to say conclusively that there are obvious differences in the way in which teachers in the classroom interact with Afro-Caribbean pupils and that these differences are influenced by ethnicity. However, the following dialogue noted during a classroom observation demonstrates how a teacher's insensitivity can result in conflict with Afro-Caribbean young people:

> The teacher was talking to the class. Whilst he wrote on the blackboard, a group of four white boys sat talking to each other in an ordinary tone of voice. The teacher, being annoyed by the noise level in the room, threw a piece of chalk at an Afro-Caribbean boy who was not being particularly noisy.
> Teacher: 'Pay attention.' (shouted)
> Teacher: (to an Asian boy) 'Could you get me that piece of chalk.'
> Peter: (Afro-Caribbean) 'Why don't you use black chalk?'
> Teacher: (turning to the researcher) 'Did you hear that? Then I would be accused of being a racist, take this for example, I was down at Lower School, I had a black girl in my class, she did something or another, I said to her, if you're not careful I'll send you back to the chocolate factory. She went home and told her parents, her dad came up to school, and decided to take the matter to the Commission for Racial Equality. It was only said in good fun, nothing malicious.'
> Keith: (Afro-Caribbean)(aggressively) 'How do we know that it's a joke, in my opinion that was a disrespectful thing to say.'
> Teacher: (raising his voice and pointing his finger at Keith) 'If I wanted to say something maliciously racist, I wouldn't have to make a joke about it. I'd say it. I've often had a joke with you, haven't I?'
> Keith: (angrily) 'Those so-called jokes were no joke, you were being cheeky. I went home and told my mum and she said that if you say it again she would come and sort you out. As for that girl, if it was my father, he wouldn't just take you to the CRE, he would also give you a good thump. My father says that a teacher should set a good example for the children, by respecting each one, whether them black or white. He says that any teacher who makes comments like that in front of a class shouldn't be in school, that's why he said to us that if a teacher ever speaks to us like that he would come up to school and sort him out.'
> Harry: 'If it was me that you said that to, I wouldn't go home and tell my parents, I would just tell you about your colour.'
> Keith: 'Teachers shouldn't make racist jokes.'

One way in which attitudes and categorisation of black pupils was fostered was through what Hargreaves calls 'informal gossip among staff'. This is an important medium in the school, since a fair proportion of teachers do not actually teach the pupils they hear talked about. Our research confirms its importance, particularly in the 'labelling' of uncooperative pupils.

How might the behaviour and attitudes of the pupils be affected by the organisation of the school and the teachers' attitudes and expectations? Hargreaves found that pupils in the lower streams were deprived of status and subsequently developed an anti-school culture which was used to gain status.

From discussion within a racially mixed group of 60 pupils, from both the fourth and fifth year, there seems to have been a consensus of opinion that the streaming system works more against black pupils. Further conversations with

16 black pupils presented the general belief that the school's organisation was against them; consequently the pupils saw very little point in trying. Furthermore, they interpreted this perception as an inevitable outcome of the school's attitude towards their colour. To the black pupils the school seemed to be seen as a 'battleground', as a hostile environment insofar as it rejects their colour and identity. Some talked to the researcher about having to put up with constant racist 'jokes' from teachers. When asked how they felt this affected their academic performance, one pupil succinctly voiced the views of the group when he said:

> You're not really given the opportunity to learn. Most of the time we're either sitting outside the Head's office or we are either fighting or we are either arguing with them. It's just we got no time, as you sit down to work they pin something on you.

The researcher found resentment, bitterness and frustration amongst the Afro-Caribbean boys towards the school — as reflected through the attitudes of certain teachers. The kind of social relationship which existed between certain teachers and this group of boys became very apparent when one examined the terms of reference used by the boys when they were referring to the teachers and themselves. It was very much an 'us' and 'them' situation. In what ways did the estranged relationship which existed between the Afro-Caribbean pupils and their teachers affect the pupils' behaviour? As in the case of the behaviour of the boys described by Hargreaves, the pupils have also developed a sub-cultural adolescent group within the school which is not only anti-school, but is also somewhat anti-white. This 'all-black' group is composed of both boys and girls: pupils from the third, fourth and fifth years. The 30 pupils or more making up the group move around together in the school during the school breaks.

Most teachers were aware of the presence of this group but unaware of the reason for its development. Even more important than this 'gang' behaviour was the deliberate assertion of 'blackness'. This was done successfully through the use of Patois. Patois was a success for the group insofar as they used it succinctly to communicate rejection of authority. Although the teachers were aware of this 'weapon', they had great difficulty in finding anything to attack it with.

In order to ascertain from the pupils some explanation of their behaviour, a group of 16 pupils was asked how they perceived their behaviour in the school. The pupils felt that they were forced into a stimulus-response situation.

School B

Focusing on School B we attempt to show that, as in School A, the nature of the relationship which existed between the Afro-Caribbean pupils and their teachers was frequently one of conflict. However, in School A this adverse relationship is not related quite so centrally to the teachers' frustrations with having to teach 'inferior' pupils. In School B the basis of this relationship may be in the teachers' particular unease with the ethnic composition of the school: an unease at being 'swamped' and having to teach 'these alien pupils'. Many teachers try to obscure the fact that they are teaching in a multiracial school. Little attempt is made to acknowledge the ethnicity of the pupils. However, what is perceived as the belligerent, aggressive, lively, gregarious character of the Afro-Caribbean pupil cannot be easily ignored by the teachers, and presents a constant reminder of the nature of the school. The following comment from a year head indicates the attitudes of some staff at the school:

> I find it very difficult to accept the immigrant people and children that I come into contact with. I cannot change my feeling because it is part of my upbringing — I feel that the English culture is being swamped. I do not see how the Asian and West Indian pupils that I am responsible for can take on English behaviour for half a day when they are at school and change to their culture when they are at home.

To what extent then do attitudes of this nature shape the Afro-Caribbean pupil-teacher relationship? Informal discussions with Afro-Caribbean pupils indicated that the pupils felt that certain teachers disrespect them on the basis of their ethnicity and they felt, therefore, that the pupil-teacher relationship was based on conflict, with the pupils attempting to play the teachers at their own 'game' in order to survive. They saw the school as condoning these teachers' attitudes.

From conversations held with Afro-Caribbean pupils it appears that many see the conflict as an inevitable response to the attitudes held by teachers towards their ethnicity. As one pupil succinctly put it, 'you then treat them without any respect because they don't give you any, so really it's just a two-way thing'. Nevertheless, the pupils did acknowledge that not all teachers held negative attitudes towards their ethnicity.

Many teachers appeared to recognise the existence of an estranged relationship, but they saw this as being inherent in the pupil with the teacher as the recipient. Conversations also suggest that categorisation of pupils' behaviour, and influence of 'informal gossip' among staff on teachers' judgments about pupils is part of the 'hidden curriculum' in this school.

We now assess the extent to which the Afro-Caribbean pupils' experience may affect their educational opportunities.

There is concern within the school about the relative underachievement of pupils — especially amongst the Afro-Caribbean group. Conversations with Afro-Caribbean pupils suggest that, like the Afro-Caribbean pupils at School A, they believe that teachers hold low academic expectations of their performance. However, unlike the pupils at School A, they saw the organisation of the school as having little influence on their educational opportunities; rather they saw the attitudes of the teachers as being paramount, concluding that the prevailing attitudes held by certain teachers would undermine the organisation of any school.

Conclusion

From observations and discussions in both schools, it seemed that the relationship between Afro-Caribbean pupils and teachers was often one of conflict and that the issue of race was frequently central to this conflict. In School A from about the third form (as the headmaster pointed out) black pupils became aware of negative attitudes they felt that the school held towards them. Similarly in School B teachers became aware of the barriers between the pupils and the teachers from the second year onwards. The perceived attitudes of teachers seemed to convince them that the school system was 'rigged' and some saw very little point in trying.

Many were still frustrated by what they saw as not 'getting on' academically. From conversations, it appeared that they were not against education per se — many of them in fact left school to go to further education. However, in school their energy was not always tapped and was sometimes directed towards disrupting the school or, as one pupil said, 'to get our own back on them for the way they have treated us'.

Allocation procedures in the two schools

The first part of this case study suggested that some sources thought that banding and setting procedures of one school might be 'rigged' to the disadvantage of Afro-Caribbean pupils. Certainly many pupils, both black and white, believed this to be the case. We now examine how far such suggestions are supported by internal evidence of ability and attainments at the crucial 'gateways' through which children pass into particular bands. We begin with a summary of allocation outcomes within the two schools.

School A

In year 1 and 2 pupils, on transfer from the junior schools, are taught in mixed ability groups, except in French and science, where there are subtle divisions on the basis of ability at the start of year 2. All pupils at this stage follow a common core curriculum, except where they are placed in a remedial group based on junior school recommendations. This group substitutes extra English for French. At the end of year 2 pupils are examined in all the subjects they have taken. However, it is their performance in English, maths, French and science which is used 'officially' to decide the teaching groups in year 3.

From year 3 onwards the school operates a banding system. Pupils are allocated to an upper or lower ability band on the basis of performance in English, maths, French and science in the second year examinations. The banding and setting of pupils is decided by the directors (ie, heads of subjects) of the above subjects. The implications of this banding system are substantial; it determines not only the curriculum followed by the two ability groups in year 3, but ultimately the options available to pupils in year 4 and subsequent public examinations taken in year 5. This is compounded by the fact that transfer between bands is very difficult because of the curricula differences between the two ability bands. Subject options are effectively reduced for the lower band pupils.

School B

On entry the 5th year at this school were allocated to two ability bands — upper and lower on transfer from the junior school. Allocation was based on ability in

English and mathematics; junior school teachers' verbal recommendation given when visited by head of year prior to transfer, and the teachers' rating of pupils' social behaviour. Pupils in both bands followed the same curriculum in year 1. On the basis of recommendations from the junior school, some pupils were assigned to a remedial group, where extra English and mathematics were substituted for French. In year 3 pupils were assigned to one of three ability bands based on their performance in the second year examinations and the subject teachers' and head of year's recommendations. The option choices are reduced for the lower band in year 4.

At the end of year 3 pupils choose a number of subjects from option blocks to study in years 4 and 5. Prior to the third year examinations, subject teachers are asked to recommend the examination level at which a pupil should be admitted to study the options chosen (ie, CSE or GCE).

For pupils in the lower band who apply for examination subjects, the teachers are asked to consider the pupils' requests. In most cases these requests are refused. Pupils are refused for various reasons including teachers' estimation of pupils' behaviour.

Group characteristics and allocation

We have noted that the assignment to sets and bands in these schools may fundamentally restrict the ability of pupils to attain credentials of specific types and levels. It is now necessary to examine some inconsistencies in the allocation procedures used in the two schools. However, it is first desirable to examine the characteristics of the intakes at the two schools.

Intake characteristics

Prior to transferring to the secondary schools, all pupils were given standardised tests for reading, and teacher ratings for comprehension and mathematics. The results from these tests, in addition to the teachers' ratings of the pupils' behaviour and recommendations for remedial help, were entered on a 'Preliminary Record Sheet', which was sent to the pupils' prospective secondary school. We have already reported that in Schools A and B the junior school recommendation was used for assigning pupils to remedial groups. In addition, School B used the assessments in English and mathematics as the criteria for allocation to bands in year 1.

Information on the mean age, mean reading age and race of pupils entering School A revealed little difference between the three groups. Afro-Caribbean pupils, with a lower mean age than Asian pupils, enter the school with a higher mean reading age. When chronological age is taken into account, Afro-Caribbean pupils also have a higher or equivalent reading age to white pupils.

Although there are differences between test scores in the upper band for pupils entering School B, they are not statistically significant. However, the mean reading age of the *total* Afro-Caribbean intake was not only higher than that of both other ethnic groups in this school, but was also higher than that of all intakes in School A.

Throughout the two schools, scores on the standardised reading test do not differentiate markedly between children of ethnic groups. Indeed, Afro-Caribbean pupils have superior scores in one school. The primary schools provide additional and more subjective ratings on the children they transfer. These include teachers' ratings of pupils' behaviour. Though measuring a quite different aspect of the same individuals, it is interesting to contrast them here.

Throughout both receiving secondary schools, Asian pupils had clearly been perceived by their former junior school teachers as being better behaved than either white or Afro-Caribbean pupils. Between the latter two groups there was little difference in ratings for those entering School A, but for School B the term 'less cooperative' was more frequently applied to Afro-Caribbean than to white pupils.

Of particular interest is that perceptions of behaviour contrast so much with findings on reading tests. How have Afro-Caribbean children learned to read so well if they are 'uncooperative'?

'Ratings of numeracy understanding' and 'ratings of comprehension and use of English language' were also provided by feeder primary schools. Further details appear in the appendix to the report and they are also mentioned in the following section on assignment to remedial groups. Broadly speaking, they suggest a very slight tendency for teachers to rank Afro-Caribbean children below those of white and Asian backgrounds in both numeracy and comprehension – but nowhere does this tendency assume statistical significance, unlike the differences in assessed behaviour.

We are faced with a dilemma. If pupils' work is assessed unimpeded by teacher judgment, the verdict seems to be more favourable for Afro-Caribbean children than if pupils' work is assessed coupled with teacher judgments on behaviour. The dilemma is familiar to many teachers who know of children with sound and measured basic capacity but who exhibit a behaviour problem which not only diminishes their own achievement but also, unless checked, those of other pupils. Our evidence does no more than to raise questions about the causes of this behaviour which may have implications for the schools' capability to promote and maintain good behaviour.

Assignment to remedial groups

In both schools certain children were recommended for remedial help on entry to the first year. There is nothing objectionable about giving pupils additional and structured help with basic skills in English language and mathematics. However, many practising teachers acknowledge that the label 'remedial' can often carry unfavourable connotations.

In School A, 33.3% of Afro-Caribbean pupils, 20% of whites and 6.7% of Asians were recommended for remedial groups. Allocations were not markedly inconsistent with junior school ratings. But in School B a different picture emerges. Here no white pupils were recommended for remedial groups, compared with 19.4% of Afro-Caribbean pupils and 7.7% of Asian pupils.

Although it is clear that junior school teachers' ratings might support a more extensive assignment of Afro-Caribbean pupils to remedial groups than of other ethnic categories, it is not clear why no white pupils should have been so assigned. It was not possible to confirm that assumptions of 'characteristic black behaviour problems' were involved in allocation procedures.

Banding at 13 plus – School A

At the end of the second year, examinations are held, pupils are then banded for the third and subsequent years on the basis of these and other assessments of their 'ability' as perceived by teachers.

White pupils were assigned half and half to the bands, children with South Asian backgrounds two-thirds upper and one-third lower, and Afro-Caribbean children two-thirds to the lower level and one-third to the upper level.

It is possible, however, that the allocation process itself might have contributed to this discrepancy between junior school ratings and allocations to ability bands at the end of the second year at the secondary school.

As an initial test of this, a selection of school reports were analysed, and an 'effort score' and 'performance' score awarded to each pupil on the basis of assessments by teachers and performance in the common second year examination. The lower the mean score, the better the perceived effort or examination performance of pupils.

Differences between the groups were slight, except perhaps for the notably higher perceived effort scores of Asian children in the upper band. These differences did not in any case assume statistical significance. However, it is noteworthy that Afro-Caribbean pupils in the lower band had the best mean performance among the groups in the sample, which would suggest a *prima facie* case for reallocation.

School B: allocation to third year bands

In School B the allocations criteria allowed the possibility of decisions being taken for 'social reasons'. The results of this process showed a slight tendency for smaller proportions of Afro-Caribbean pupils to be allocated to the upper band.

Even apparently equal distribution of allocational opportunity may disguise within itself further disadvantaging. The 'effort' and 'performance' scores for each ethnic group within each band were constructed in the manner outlined for School A; again performance scores are the product of common end-of-year examinations.

We found that while both 'performance' and 'effort' scores were as may be expected for white and Asian pupils placed in lower bands, no such consistency was apparent for Afro-Caribbean pupils. Indeed, the latter group had lower mean scores for the lower band than the middle. We found no explanation of the significantly higher scores of Afro-Caribbean pupils in the upper band compared to other groups therein. This was possibly, in part, a result of allocation on non-cognitive criteria, rather than on criteria reflecting 'ability'.

Comments written in internal reports produced to determine the allocation of pupils appear to confirm that, for Afro-Caribbean pupils, behavioural perceptions may act as a major determinant of placement.

Examination entries

We conclude with details of the examination entries within and between ethnic groups.

Table 1: Schools A and B: Examination entries by ethnic group

	Asian	Afro-Caribbean	White
SCHOOL A			
5 or more CSEs	69.0%	78.9%	80.0%
1 or more 'O' level	58.5%	26.3%	41.9%
5 or more 'O' levels	20.5%	5.3%	24.5%
SCHOOL B			
5 or more CSEs	65.2%	78.0%	57.6%
1 or more 'O' level	46.7%	22.2%	34.8%
5 or more 'O' levels	16.3%	2.7%	18.5%

Table 1 shows the marked decline in the relative position of the groups of Afro-Caribbean pupils during their five years of secondary education. They entered the two schools with reading ages on a par with or higher than those attained by the other two groups; and finish up in both schools with only one child each entered for five or more 'O' levels.

The examination results eventually attained are consistent with these entries — Afro-Caribbean young people in the two schools were significantly less likely to achieve 'O' levels, thus potentially decreasing their occupational prospects. Table 2 shows the examination results achieved at the end of the fifth year.

Table 2: Schools A and B: Fifth year examination results by ethnic group (all pupils: categories are *not* exclusive)

	Asian	Afro-Caribbean	White
SCHOOL A			
5 or more CSEs	58.6%	57.9%	62.5%
1 or more 'O' levels or CSE grade 1s	41.4%	15.8%	41.3%
5 or more 'O' levels or CSE grade 1s	10.3%	0	9.0%
SCHOOL B			
5 or more CSEs	58.7%	66.7%	50.5%
1 or more 'O' levels or CSE grade 1s	35.9%	25.0%	32.6%
5 or more 'O' levels or CSE grade 1s	14.1%	2.8%	14.7%

Disciplinary procedures

The study has suggested that the relationship between teachers and Afro-Caribbean pupils within the two schools was often antagonistic. It was suggested that this influenced the teachers' judgments of pupils' ability and some Afro-Caribbean pupils may have been placed in inappropriate ability groups and examination sets, thus restricting their opportunities. There is also a suggestion that this relationship may precipitate certain sanctions taken by the school. The ultimate sanction is that of removing a pupil from the school.

Both schools use similar disciplinary procedures for dealing with 'unacceptable behaviour' by pupils. Concentrating on the year group chosen for this study, we looked at sanctions taken against pupils whose behaviour was deemed 'unacceptable' by the schools.

Suspensions

In School A a number of pupils had committed a criminal act of arson against the school which resulted in one Asian boy and three white boys being expelled and placed in other schools; the remaining pupils suspended in this period (four Afro-Caribbean and two white) were suspended because of their 'unacceptable behaviour' towards the teachers.

In 1983 this school modified its organisation to make special provision for 'disruptive' pupils, known as an 'on-site unit'. This unit allows pupils deemed disruptive in the classroom to remain in school — although withdrawn from selected or all lessons. At present the unit is not adequately equipped to enable the pupils to have access to the full range of curricula activity offered in the mainstream school and admission to this unit may therefore reduce the pupils' educational opportunities.

Thus suspension and eventual expulsion of pupils from the school for 'unacceptable behaviour' towards teachers is one way in which the school deals with pupils — predominantly Afro-Caribbean — who come into conflict with their teachers. The behaviour of teachers may make suspension and expulsion of some pupils more likely. One teacher remarked about another:

> He's the one who causes that problem with 'John' and will continue to have problems with John, because he's rude to him, and John unlike a lot of pupils will be respectful but he demands respect from the teachers. A lot of pupils just ignore it and serve their time but not John plus the fact that he is too big [in stature] to insult. What happened recently with his suspension was that Mr L insulted him, so he was rude back, and he got suspended of course, because he swore back.

The task of proving an act of 'unacceptable behaviour' towards teachers can be tinted with a degree of controversy. When the case is presented to the governors, it normally consists of the teacher's word against the child's. Frequently it is the teacher's perception of the pupil's behaviour that will be influential.

One of the researcher's first impressions of School B — later confirmed as familiarity with the school developed — was the teachers' and, to a certain extent, the pupils' continuous reference to indiscipline. This emphasis on indiscipline occurred in staff meetings, heads of departments' meetings and year heads' meetings.

A special support unit was first set up in 1979 as a withdrawal unit for disruptive pupils. With directions from a new headmaster, the unit has quite recently changed its aims and composition. However, it is still the case (as it was with the special unit) that pupils placed in this unit do not necessarily have access to the full curricula activity offered in the mainstream because of lack of facilities.

Although an equal number of pupils from each ethnic group were placed in the unit for this particular year group, the Afro-Caribbean pupils accounted for under 20% of the population. Our inquiries suggest that the school was more likely to debar disruptive Afro-Caribbean pupils from the school temporarily or permanently. One of the teachers who works in the unit suggested that Afro-Caribbean pupils were normally placed in the unit with the sole purpose of using it as a 'half-way' house for permanent exclusion.

In School B over half the pupils who entered the school in 1979 and were subsequently suspended or expelled from the school were Afro-Caribbeans, which meant that 23.2% of Afro-Caribbean pupils who entered the school in 1979 were suspended and 9.3% of the group were referred to the educational psychologist. None of the pupils expelled from the school in the fourth year was offered alternative educational provision.

Referrals

Table 3 shows the referral pattern to the psychological service for this school over two years.

Table 3: Referrals described by ethnic group membership 1982-83

Type of problem		Asian	Afro-Caribbean	White
Behaviour —	conduct	3	9	12
	personal	1	0	7
Learning —	slow	1	0	3
	specific	0	0	1

Discussion

The ethnographic case study of only two schools has presented evidence indicating that the low achievement of some of their ethnic minority adolescents is linked with the procedures of the schools, and that these procedures may be causal or at least powerful determinants of pupil effort, performance and attitude. We emphasise again that there is no suggestion that these schools, their teachers or their pupils are representative. Equally, there is no suggestion that they are unrepresentative.

Although the evidence offered in this chapter is more narrowly based and more 'subjective' than that of other parts of the report, it has the merit of offering a very much closer picture of detailed procedures of schools than our national survey permits. Notwithstanding the differences in breadth and approach, we find considerable compatibility: the study of the two schools accords with much of the experience recorded nationally. By juxtaposing this material with our survey data we believe that we can offer a further and linked perspective on the educational and vocational development of ethnic minority adolescents.

The evidence offered suggests that within the classroom, in allocation to sets, streams or bands and in examination entries, complex processes may be involved which can disadvantage black young people, and in this study particularly those of Afro-Caribbean origin. These conclusions are compatible with evidence available from other sources.

It is probable that assignment of pupils to groups undertaking a lower standard of work than they are capable of and entering them for lower level examinations or no examinations at all can affect their level of school-leaving qualifications. So can excluding them altogether from particular subjects or from their school. It is also apparent that pupils or groups particularly subject to these processes may not attain examination results which reflect their ability and potential. Comparisons of public examination results must be interpreted with care or they may reinforce the processes which bring about observed differences in attainment.

It is tempting but over-simplistic to blame teachers. We have tried to report both their difficulties and their perceptions.

Possible racial disadvantage is often seen as an individual matter to be handled by informal and individual means, and not within the official structure of the school. Yet if pupils face disciplinary procedures arising in part out of racial issues they are confronted by the full authority structure of the school, wherein individual teachers may be given full support by their colleagues at all levels.

We have discussed informal gossip among teachers but not similar gossip amongst pupils or communities at large. All teachers know that classroom incidents and disciplinary procedures are a major focus of conversation among school children. This knowledge is rapidly and widely spread, particularly if children have, or believe they have, been treated unfairly. If pupils discern a repeated pattern of injustice, discontent may well become general among the pupils affected and come to have a lowering effect on the whole life and work of the school.

6. The careers service

The national context

The decline in vacancies notified to careers officers and the rise in Manpower Services Commission provision have greatly affected the operations of careers services, but they continue to have a critical influence on the placement of black school-leavers. We thought it necessary, therefore, to investigate aspects of their role and of the underlying policies and procedures which might affect the treatment they accord their clients. The researchers have also been in contact with careers officers from services other than of the project authorities: these too have contributed to the information and quotation in this chapter.

All LEAs with an ethnic minority population of more than 10,000 were contacted in May 1983, except those in which the research team was already working. We sent a standard letter to a named principal careers officer in each authority, and followed up the reply with a more flexible approach seeking specific information on the use of statistics on ethnic minority young people.

The statistical and record-keeping situation is changing: two authorities informed us that they intended to develop ethnic monitoring with the implementation of new computing systems. We have also included information from one authority that had produced rather detailed ethnic statistics in previous years, but did not do so in the survey year due to the introduction of a new computing system.

Yet another of our project authorities had not previously collected data as it was 'not official policy' and 'not required by law'. The officer in charge of statistics also stated that 'We don't do that kind of thing here — it wouldn't be right to ask'. However, after several interviews the assistant principal officer said that 'We don't want to be accused of discrimination, so we have moved to a system of simple and positive identification'. This system was to be introduced in 1982-3, and was:

W = West Indian type
A = Asian type
O = Others

The rationale behind this coding was simplicity, and that it 'links up with the way employers view young people'.

Inevitably the details we have given in some ways underestimate the proportion of careers services which engage in ethnic classification. In other ways we overestimate the extent of classification, for we have included county authorities when only one or two town offices are involved and the remainder of careers offices disregard ethnic record-keeping.

In some authorities, the collection of ethnic records seemed to have little evident beneficial effect on policy. Careers services which do not analyse their own records or which keep records in a difficult-to-interpret form are unlikely to benefit. A few careers services neither keep ethnic records nor make any of their statistics available. Such a procedure poses questions about the accountability of a service of such importance to young people.

The distinction between equality of opportunity and equality of outcome applies particularly to the work of careers services. Officers may offer interviews equally to black and white young people of equivalent qualifications, but employers may accept them unequally. In this case the careers service is offering equality of opportunities, but not providing equality of outcomes – and there may be procedures which can be undertaken to diminish that inequality. Officers may even offer interviews unequally themselves, perhaps through the application of stereotypes about the capabilities of young people with particular characteristics. It is hard to see how either of these processes may be easily detected without some form of systematic monitoring. A lack of monitoring may contribute to a lack of awareness of racial disadvantage by disguising the processes which maintain it.

We suggest that in some areas inadequate presentation of statistics and the later entry of many black young people may serve to divert careers officers' attention from the severity of racial disadvantage in the labour market, which may become statistically more apparent for young people a little older than those traditionally the major focus of careers service provision. It may be for these reasons that we were able to find a Section 11 funded careers officer with special responsibilities for ethnic minorities in a borough who was prepared to state and believe that 'There is no discrimination in ..., except perhaps employers want Asians because they work harder'. Careers teachers interviewed in this authority disagreed, suggesting that particular employers certainly operated racially discriminatory recruitment policies to the detriment of black young people.

Project authorities, careers statistics and careers officers

We follow our discussion of the national context of the careers service with information from our own work in project authorities and with associated statistics on the distribution and destinations of ethnic minority young people. Careers officers were interviewed in every authority.

Fifth year destinations

Information from Bradford and Hounslow revealed a marked preference for staying on at school amongst ethnic minorities when contrasted with their white peers. This difference was particularly acute in Hounslow, where a higher proportion of whites were seeking employment (62% of white boys and 52% of white girls), and a higher proportion of ethnic minorities staying at school (40% of black boys and 41% of black girls). This suggests distinct strategies for realising careers aspirations specific to a relatively high employment area within a wider economy suffering widespread unemployment. However, the ethnic composition of the Hounslow minority population may also be relevant, not only through origin but also by self-selection. Some primary settlement did take place in this borough, in part through its proximity to Heathrow. But most new arrivals come from other, poorer parts of London rather than the Indian sub-continent. We may be considering a class-stratified subset of the ethnic groups in question. The East African origins of many might also perhaps be relevant, when compared with the Mirpuri and other Pakistani origins of many in Bradford.

Fifth year pupils seeking work

Tables 4 and 5 again provide a contrast between the two boroughs. Due to the small number involved in the Hounslow schools, these figures have not been divided by sex.

Table 4: Bradford pupils reaching ssla and leaving for employment (not transferred)

	Boys		Girls	
	White	Black	White	Black
Entering first employment	34%	6%	29%	10%
Entering YOP	41%	34%	40%	22%
Registered as unemployed	20%	29%	19%	29%
Not registered	5%	31%	12%	39%

Table 5: Hounslow fifth year pupils leaving for employment (not transferred)

	White	Asian
Entering first employment	62%	7%
Entering YOP	9%	29%
Registered as unemployed	9%	24%
Not registered	14%	36%

An immediate contrast is between the relative success of whites in finding work in Hounslow as compared with Bradford — evidently a function of their local economies. However, ethnic minority young people appear to be equivalently unsuccessful in obtaining work in the two areas, though the Hounslow numbers are so low as to be virtually uninterpretable.

Non-registration presents additional problems of interpretation. Discussions with careers officers in Bradford suggested no easy explanations. Despite the existence of some outreach work, it was not necessarily popular as there was a reticence attached to seeking out the unregistered if one has no work to offer them. It should be noted that non-registration was almost as high amongst boys as girls, so traditional role expectations cannot present sufficient explanation even if such were in any case a likely resolution. Further, it does not seem likely that family businesses are providing full employment for the ethnic minority unregistered disproportionately to their numbers. A predominant form of business is the retail outlet. The relative number of outlets in Bradford is approximately proportionate to the size of the ethnic minority electorate, and their turnover almost certainly disproportionately small.

In view of other research findings that young people of South Asian origin are no more prone to non-registration than others, a most likely explanation for many of the non-registered is a slight delay in registration. This may coincide with our later suggestion that there was also a slight delay in making use of the Youth Opportunities Programme. There is also perhaps the quite simple explanation that the careers services had merely lost contact with some of these young people.

Table 4 also suggests that black youth in Bradford were considerably less likely to enter YOP than their white counterparts, a destination for which careers office statistics are likely to be accurate. This may again simply highlight the 'snapshot' nature of destination figures. Among whites, 1,546 reportedly entered YOP according to the table. According to MSC statistics, places filled in February and April 1983 were 1,250 and 875 respectively. For ethnic minorities, the figures from the same three sources were 110, 98, 127. Possibly, white young people were taking advantage of YOP provision at an earlier time, although this is again speculative.

Sixth form destinations

Table 6: Bradford sixth form pupils leaving for employment (not transferred)

	Boys		Girls	
	White	Black	White	Black
Registered as unemployed	48%	42%	23%	28%
Entering first employment	34%	7%	42%	4%
Entering YOP	13%	4%	12%	12%
Not registered	6%	48%	22%	55%

Once again, the question of non-registration is raised, and the same hypotheses can be presented.

In contrast to the situation in Bradford, sixth form leavers from our two schools in Hounslow did not appear to have fared so badly (Table 7). Their comparative advantage appears even greater when one sees the type of job they attained (see below).

Table 7: Hounslow sixth form pupils leaving school for employment

	White	Asian
Entering first employment	83%	63%
Entering YOP	8%	3%
Registered as unemployed	4%	7%
Not registered	4%	27%

Employment entered

Table 8 shows the first job attained by all Bradford leavers, categorised by race and type of training. The figures show *prima facie* evidence of discrimination in employment practices within Bradford. Many of the possible mechanisms operating have been outlined in a study of recruitment to apprenticeships in Birmingham, a study of especial relevance to Bradford given the continuing prevalence of this mode of training within the locality. A number of ethnic minority young people in our research cohort had ambitions which would be most easily fulfilled through the attainment of an apprenticeship. Most failed to achieve them.

Table 8: First employment entered

	Boys		Girls	
	White	Black	White	Black
Apprenticeship	34%	12%	7%	--
Professional training	2%	4%	2%	4%
Clerical	8%	8%	36%	35%
Training – 12 months or more	9%	4%	9%	4%
Training – 8 weeks-12 months	15%	27%	20%	23%
Unskilled	32%	46%	26%	35%

Bradford careers officers reported no discouragement of black youngsters from applying for apprenticeships. One said: 'We send them for the interviews, but they don't seem to get the jobs.' They also strongly denied discouraging sixth-form entry – which while furthering academic aspirations can preclude entry to age-specific apprenticeship schemes.

The statistics for Hounslow certainly *appear* to present a different picture from Bradford, though they are not directly comparable as we have compared occupations only for sixth formers, and do not have the detailed information on training available to the Bradford careers service.

From the limited evidence we have available for Hounslow, there is not *prima facie* evidence of differential job status between Asians and white youths. Seventeen of the Asian sixth-form leavers had in fact entered skilled non-manual jobs compared with only eight of the white leavers. Two Asian leavers were in semi- or unskilled jobs compared with six white leavers. However, the data is puzzling; most of the Asians who had left for employment were girls. The boys had not, apparently, entered the job market.

Earlier research has noted the high extent to which Asian young people in a neighbouring borough were keen to stay on at school (80% even of 'working class families') and enter higher education in 1979. Indeed, only 24% of this cohort of sixth-formers in the entire borough left full-time education. Our own research gives us no reason to suppose that circumstances have altered. Given the small numbers of sixth-formers leaving our Hounslow schools for work, it appears that the vast majority will be hoping to continue their education.

Type of YOP undertaken
Careers office figures from Birmingham showed that ethnic minorities in Birmingham, as in Bradford, were less likely to choose YOP than whites. However, within YOP, they were more likely to be placed in Short Training Courses and Work Introduction Courses than white youngsters. Conversely, the latter were more

likely to undertake Work Experience on Employers Premises (WEEP). It is possible that WEEP was more likely to lead to the prospect of a job than other provisions — it was certainly more likely to involve sustained contact with a potential employer and experience of a genuine workplace.

Information and policy

Another aspect of the careers service in which we have taken an active interest is the extent to which posts were allocated with special responsibility for ethnic minority groups, and any external funding for these.

Hounslow appointed a Section 11 funded officer with special responsibilities towards ethnic minority groups in March 1980. Her role was primarily that of an ordinary officer, with a full caseload selected without reference to ethnicity from two comprehensive schools. She assumed special responsibility for the small number of students attending the Schools Language (withdrawal) Unit and the English Foundation Course at Hounslow Borough College liaised with the local CRC and cognate bodies. To that extent her appointment escaped the criticism of 'funding inexplicitness' sometimes levelled at many uses of Section 11 funding in other sectors of education.

This officer worked to an official view that 'young people from ethnic minorities obtained, without undue difficulty, opportunities for training and employment commensurate with other young people possessing the same academic and personal qualities . . . therefore there appeared no overriding need to treat the ethnic minorities any differently'.

This view was based on evidence derived from unemployment register statistics. Given the borough policy, and the fact that the specialist officer herself looked after the 'problem cases', there was thus little perceived need for any in-service training of other officers.

Bradford had three specialist posts and also a centrally funded 'outreach' worker. Two worked mainly with 'ESL groups' in upper schools and the senior Language Centre. The third also had a small caseload of a similar nature, an administrative role and a small in-service function. He also talked to specially constituted groups in schools without benefit of another specialist officer. This latter act could sometimes have evident effect, according to the testimony of another officer. At a school with a voluntary referral system, she was 'deluged' with enquiries from an 'ESL group' the day after his talk, a contrast to her contention that ethnic minority pupils in general and more recent arrivals in particular were normally more reluctant to put themselves forward for advisory interviews.

The in-service function of the specialist officer was evidenced in interviews with other careers officers by their awareness of the statistical position of minority school leavers in Bradford. They were, however, less certain of what, if any, implications this posed for their own role as careers advisers. Nevertheless, this awareness of possible racial disadvantage in the labour market seemed to assist officers in the borough towards care in the statements they made about young people from minority groups. While officers did talk about 'over-aspiration' and 'unrealistic ambitions' at times, such statements tended to be qualified. Thus it might be specified that 'some parents' were over-ambitious for their children and reasoned explanations given, rather than a group of young people being categorised together in a somewhat dismissive fashion.

The officers interviewed in Birmingham also with an 'outreach' worker were also, on the whole, more careful about making generalisations than some in other authorities. Birmingham, like Bradford, prepares careers statistics analysing the labour market position of minorities, while publications and internal memoranda issued by the service offer additional commentary and information.

The genesis of local policies and approaches is difficult to determine. Publications and statistics to some extent provide a context for policy and a focus for some in-service training and discussion, though a specialist officer with an active commitment to in-service noted that this is 'certainly not a prime function — I've only got limited time and resources'. Training officers and those in senior administrative positions also have an in-service role, but we have seen little evidence that this was exercised to the specific benefit of ethnic minorities. Indeed, our impression of several senior officers was that they too were in the position of learners rather than teachers in this field. Where developments are occurring, the pressure may come from elements outside the service: 'The push to make things happen here has come from having people in posts with a race training responsibility elsewhere in the authority — posts contingent upon a recently introduced Equal Opportunities Policy. To be fair, they've opened my eyes.'

The statistical evidence sometimes presented also sheds little light on the precise loci of disadvantage. Did careers officers themselves have a role in diverting ethnic minority clients away from prime employment opportunities? Or were the conditions of the labour market itself the major cause of disadvantage?

Careers services themselves were rarely able to provide answers to such questions to their own satisfaction. Indeed, one officer claimed that 'There has been a concentration on the deficiency model — we have been unwilling or unprepared to accept what is going on out there in the labour market'. The result may have been a perpetuation of systems related to the individual client, but little analysis of what happens in referral for vacancies or employers' selection.

Only the data on recruitment to MSC provision in Birmingham (also collected in Bradford) began to approach these issues, and here the picture was sometimes found to be disturbing. Some careers officers were concerned that ethnic minority groups appeared to be disproportionately allocated to forms of provision which may be less promising in their eventual employment outcomes for young people.

A potential resolution of this dilemma was the extension of monitoring procedures to assess allocation to vacancies by the careers service and employment outcomes determined by employers. In the former case, officers could then be more directly faced with the implications of their own systems and decisions. In the latter, the service could attempt to provide employers with the evidence of the waste of talent arising from their procedures; though officers were well aware that the careers service depends upon maintaining close relationships with such employers.

In one authority the extension of monitoring was under active consideration. Plans were proposed which went some way towards enhancing the quality of data available to inform decision-making. One officer involved stated, 'Frankly, this is what I think my job ought to be.' He also noted that the implementation of such measures required that sufficient finance and manpower be made available. As we have seen, there were few specialist careers officers for minority groups, and even where they existed they had other roles: 'So long as I'm case-loaded, I'm going to find it very difficult to be effective in that area.'

For in the two project schools at least, very few ethnic minority young people left education at a time when they remained clearly the statutory concern of the careers service. As unemployment amongst minority groups has consistently been shown to be comparatively more severe throughout the nation in times of recession, it was perhaps to be expected that evidence of racial disadvantage would also be more elusive in a local labour market which is relatively flourishing.

Stereotyping?

There was sometimes a tendency for careers officers to exhibit 'anglocentric' judgments of incompletely understood customs and procedures. One officer spoke of judgmental talk about girls being 'doomed' to 'hateful' arranged marriages which would inevitably be 'loveless'. On case-notes there was sometimes reference to 'very close family, traditional', 'traditional Asian family' (we doubted the accuracy of the inferred conceptual category). There was also concern in some offices about the extent to which 'Asian girls' would not seek work — 'they' were supposed to settle down and raise a family, though there is evidence that the female activity rate for Sikh and Hindu women in the British labour market is similar to that for whites.

There was also a tendency for some officers to feel free to generalise about minorities. One example arose in an interview where an officer claimed that 'Asian boys were too ambitious' — only aiming at the traditional professions such as law and medicine — and shortly afterwards claimed that they lacked ambition: 'There are the jobs if only they go prepared to travel to the centre, but of course they will not leave their little haven of security.' The same officer said of West Indians that 'the very bright are very bright, but generally they're not so bright — not good academically really'. In contrast he could not generalise about whites — a 'range of attitudes'.

Given the virtual non-existence of structured in-service education programmes for careers officers within the authorities studied, it was not surprising to find out that knowledge often came through unsystematic and sporadic means.

Stereotypes may be of concern in themselves but they assumed greater significance when we received hearsay reports from office conversations of the ways they might narrow the opportunities offered to pupils of minority groups in various ways. An example would be the reported pre-selection of 'suitable' opportunities: 'Oh I couldn't offer her that, not for an Asian girl!'

Summary

In this chapter on the careers service we have argued that the form and manner of the available statistics may serve to direct the attention of the service from the severity of racial disadvantage in the labour market. We have attempted to re-analyse evidence to indicate the true position more clearly. This has shown a wide range of differences in an overall pattern of disadvantage. The enthusiasm of black young people to continue in full-time education in the hope of betterment is a recurring feature. The efficacy of this varies with some advantage being shown for some categories — eg, Asian girls in Hounslow. Another feature is the delayed or total non-registration of black young people for YTS and the greater tendency of those who do register to enter schemes other than the attractive WEEP versions.

More generally we have portrayed the gaps in knowledge and understanding on the part of all participants — officers at various levels, teachers and clients — all bringing their preconceptions and stereotypes to the process of guidance. The case for more effective monitoring and in-service training seems very strong.

7. Destinations and examinations at 16+

Examinations

Entries to public examinations

We begin our consideration of the examination results and likely destinations of cohort members by looking at entries to public examinations in the fifth year.

Table 9 shows the number of examinations entered for at both CSE and 'O' level. Afro-Caribbean boys have been entered in all for fewer examinations than others. Afro-Caribbean girls were also slightly less likely to be entered for nine or more examinations.

Table 9: Examination entries at 'O' level, 16+ and CSE

	Asian	Afro-Caribbean	White
BOYS			
None	3.1%	9.7%	11.5%
1-5	28.1%	34.7%	18.9%
6-8	37.5%	52.8%	52.7%
9 or more	29.9%	2.8%	17.1%
GIRLS			
None	6.5%	2.9%	7.4%
1-5	20.4%	25.7%	20.6%
6-8	44.1%	65.7%	41.9%
9 or more	29.0%	5.7%	30.1%

In Chapter 5 we provided a detailed description of the allocation processes affecting Afro-Caribbean pupils in two Midlands schools. It is possible that similar processes operate in other schools attended by members of the cohort; if this is the case, the lower level of examination entries for Afro-Caribbean pupils may be attributed in part to the failure of schools to provide adequately for the academic potential of their black pupils.

A possible contributory explanation of examination entry differences lies in the overall procedures of schools. Some of the project schools were of the kind characterised as 'CSE schools', in which few pupils are entered for 'O' level and the level of teaching is oriented towards CSE examinations. The level of entries also varies between local authorities.

Our findings appeared to suggest that some schools were not stretching their pupils sufficiently. In this we are also reminded that some of our schools, particularly some of those attended by many Afro-Caribbean pupils, have been subject to disruptive amalgamation procedures.

Passes in public examinations

In Table 10 we provide details of examination outcomes in the project schools.

Table 10: Grades in fifth year by local authority (in % rounded to nearest whole number)

	Asian			Afro-Caribbean			White		
	none	5(+) high	1-4 high	none	5(+) high	1-4 high	none	5(+) high	1-4 high
Bedford	11	7	7	0	0	15	6	17	30
Birmingham	6	6	30	0	13	25	6	13	25
Bradford	4	8	33	*			15	22	20
Ealing	0	43	33	8	0	33	8	24	40
Hounslow	0	30	10	*			3	16	45
ILEA		*		11	9	33	13	6	35

* denotes cells containing single figure numbers of pupils

Table 10 shows that within our cohort Afro-Caribbean young people in ILEA and Birmingham had very slightly higher examination attainments than pupils of other ethnic groups — as our four pupils of South Asian ethnic origin in ILEA achieved very poor results. There was also little difference between the performance of Asian and white pupils in Bradford and Birmingham schools. In Bedford the white pupils did rather better than those from ethnic minorities, while in our West London schools it seems to be Asian young people who are very slightly ahead of the rest.

It is these kinds of subtleties which lead us to regard Table 11 with some suspicion. It presents a collation of examination results in the manner of the 'Rampton Report' on *West Indian Children in our Schools*. That report was for all school leavers in six LEAs. Despite this major difference, the distributions of grades we record between ethnic groups are fairly similar. We have a lower proportion of pupils with no graded results, which we suspect may have arisen in part from sample loss due to absentees, particularly among Easter leavers within our cohort. Nevertheless, the similarities, including a suggestion of 'West Indian underachievement', do not appear to be replicated at local levels within the cohort, for the picture of relatively high attainment among Asian young people has arisen mainly in schools in the two west London authorities.

Also worthy of note in Table 11 is the attainment of Afro-Caribbean girls, which does not differ greatly from other girls. Although certain other studies have suggested that Afro-Caribbean girls 'do better' than boys, we would not wish to assert this with any degree of certainty from our own cohort. The small number of these girls and their different distribution in schools make such a conclusion unreliable.

Table 11: Grades in fifth year GCE 'O' level and CSE examinations, by sex (%)

	Asian	Afro-Caribbean	White
BOYS			
No graded result	4.7	9.7	13.5
No high grades	45.3	61.1	37.8
1 to 4 high grades	26.6	23.6	35.8
5 or more high grades	23.4	5.6	12.8
GIRLS			
No graded result	6.5	2.9	8.1
No high grades	49.5	48.6	39.7
1 to 4 high grades	30.1	37.1	30.1
5 or more high grades	14.0	11.4	22.1
ALL			
No graded result	5.7	7.5	10.9
No high grades	47.8	57.0	38.7
1 to 4 high grades	28.7	28.0	33.1
5 or more high grades	17.8	7.5	17.3

Destinations

The 1983 respondents

The majority of 1983 respondents had stayed on into the sixth form at their schools, with ethnic minority young people being particularly likely to choose this option. Nearly two-thirds of Asians (62.5%) and 56.7% of Afro-Caribbeans had stayed on compared with 44.3% of whites.

Among the young people of South Asian ethnic origin continuing in education, only 10% of the girls go to colleges of further education compared with 38% of the boys. An opposing discrepancy exists for Afro-Caribbean young people, matched to a lesser extent by similar choices among whites.

Explanations for such differences may include the characteristics of the sample, the cultural characteristics of each group, their aspirations and their attainments. It may be, for example, that the slightly lower examination performance of white and Afro-Caribbean boys in our sample compared to their female peers affects their ability to pass the barriers of entry to another institution; whereas their schools may be very willing to retain into the sixth form those boys who wish to stay on and whom the school regards as desirable. Certainly four Afro-Caribbean boys stated that they remained at school because they could not go to college, a number which could have tripled the proportion at college had they succeeded. No whites and only two Asian boys declared this reason for entering the sixth form.

Amongst girls of Asian ethnic origin, they or their parents possibly perceive schools as more desirable environments than colleges, which may be perceived as more permissive and in any case further from home. In this context it is also worth noting the proportion of girls in our sample from single-sex schools, some of whom attend on account of their parents' express wish for this kind of education to be available for their daughters.

A stark difference is apparent when destinations of respondents no longer in full-time education are revealed. At the time of the survey, no ethnic minority boys were in full-time jobs whatsoever, and only 14 girls. This could be because a higher proportion of the 'motivated' minority group young people stayed in the school or college. The difference between the destinations of the young people of the ethnic groupings is highly significant statistically even though extremely small numbers are involved. Bearing in mind our earlier hesitation about applying significance tests to educational research, we shall explore the characteristics of the young people involved in detail in later chapters. Meanwhile, Table 12 serves to illustrate the basic differences.

Table 12: Destinations of leavers, by sex

	Asian	Afro-Caribbean	White
BOYS			
Unemployed	66.7%	50.0%	15.9%
In full-time work	0	0	77.3%
Other	33.3%	50.0%	6.8%
GIRLS			
Unemployed	22.2%	20.0%	14.0%
In full-time work	66.7%	20.0%	72.0%
Other	11.1%	60.0%	14.0%

The 'other' category in Table 12 is complex, being composed of those in MSC provision, those in part-time work and/or study and a very small number of young people who may be confining themselves to domestic activity. This will be explored again later, but it is worth regarding part-time education as a 'destination' for the purposes of this chapter. A high proportion of the young leavers were undertaking part-time studies, and there were again striking and significant differences between ethnic minority young people and their white peers. The former were more likely to be studying, but on their own account or on an MSC scheme for unemployed young people. The latter group, when studying, was doing so as part of their paid employment.

Summary

The chapter has shown that overall white pupils are most likely to be entered for and to succeed in 'O' level and CSE examinations and Afro-Caribbean boys least likely. There seems to be a range of factors suggesting unrecognised academic potential linked with school expectations, traditions and ethos — both overt and covert — rather than an intellectual inadequacy.

These differences in examination performance do not necessarily reflect the abilities of the young people. And, as levels of attainment differed between and within local authorities, the order of attainment between groups did not remain constant. It is also notable that the majority of Afro-Caribbean pupils within the cohort were attending a small number of schools in only two of the six LEAs. Furthermore, the ethnographic study of two additional schools in a further LEA suggests that certain special factors might operate to the disadvantage of Afro-Caribbean pupils in some schools. If teachers hold views antagonistic to particular racial groups *and* if in any resulting conflict such teachers are supported by the authority structure of their schools, the consequences are likely to be detrimental to the attainments of most if not all pupils of that group. If racial prejudice operates among teachers, low examination achievements could be even less adequate than usual as an indication of a young person's occupational capacity.

Differential staying-on patterns were also demonstrated — black young people being more likely to remain in continuing education. This was particularly true of further education participation — blacks being twice as likely as whites to go to college, especially Asian boys and Afro-Caribbean girls. Black examination achievement in further education was markedly higher proportionally than in the sixth form. Black children also had a higher rate of participation in part-time education after school. Not surprisingly, the employment record of black children is lower — which may partly be due to the high incidence of staying-on among the most motivated young people.

8. Young people in continuing education

Future destinations

We begin our analysis of the 221 respondents at school and college by considering their intended destinations after leaving their current educational institutions. This may place in context their reasons for participating in continuing education and their choices of courses. We first asked the group when they thought they would leave school or college. We found significant differences between groups classified by sex and by ethnicity. Young people of Asian ethnic origin and Afro-Caribbean girls were least likely to be thinking of leaving in 1983, though a further four of the latter group would leave if they found a job. Overall it is, however, notable that only 14 of the 221 respondents would leave in this situation. It is also worthy of note that almost a quarter of the Asian young people were possibly envisaging spending three years in further education or school sixth forms, compared with less than 10% of white students.

We found differences for the 112 respondents intending to leave their school or college in 1983. Only one of the college students was intending to transfer to another college, but over one-third of the school leavers were expecting to be at a college of further education. Indeed, over half of the black school leavers responding thought they were likely to be at college in 1983-4. In contrast, nearly three-quarters of the whites thought they were most likely to be at work. We also offered the group the option of responding to the category 'staying at home and not seeking work'; none wished to do this.

Overall, about half of the group wanted to continue their education after leaving school or college, while the other half hoped to go out to work. We again gave students the option of responding to the category 'stay at home', but it was not taken up.

A greater proportion of black students wanted to go to college or university and seemed more likely than white respondents to choose a college of further education in order to fulfil this ambition. Few white students in colleges were intending to go on to higher education, while white lower sixth leavers were also unlikely to expect to go to colleges of further education.

Looking for work?

One-third of respondents in continuing education claimed to have applied for full-time jobs or apprenticeships by the summer of 1983. White and Afro-Caribbean students were significantly more likely to have applied for jobs than young people of South Asian ethnic origin. Over half of the former groups had looked for work, but less than a quarter of the latter had applied for any jobs at all. Within the white and Afro-Caribbean groups there were few differences here between boys and girls, though Afro-Caribbean boys and white girls were slightly more likely to have made applications. This coincides with these groups' slightly greater tendencies to express a wish to leave to look for work than their opposite sex counterparts. Amongst the girl respondents with Asian family backgrounds, less than 10% had made applications, compared to over 40% of boys. It seems that many of our respondents have thus actively been seeking jobs, and it is possible that some would not have remained in education had they been able to find work to their satisfaction.

Almost half of the group were prepared to admit the possibility that they might not find a job at all, and almost as many that they might go on a government scheme for the unemployed. In both these cases black respondents were rather more likely to be pessimistic about their prospects, as almost three-quarters of whites both felt sure they would get work and would not consider training schemes. It may be that the preference for continued education by black young people was a consequence of their greater uncertainty about the labour market and a way of avoiding exposure to failure. Yet almost half the respondents also felt that they might have missed opportunities by continuing their education, that education might make no difference to their prospects, and that they might ultimately have to accept any job they could get.

These uncertainties must be considered in conjunction with the opposing notions that education would help them find a better job, and that they would only look for jobs they really wanted. Only just over 10% of respondents actually disagreed with these statements — with no significant differences between ethnic groups. However, their concurrence with these sentiments must be seen in part as agreement with an ideal: young people should not necessarily be regarded as unduly optimistic, particularly when taking their other reservations into account.

Reasons for continuing education

The young people's reasons for staying at school or going to college have been implicit in the previous sections of this chapter. Many wanted to enter higher education, many believed that education would assist them to get a job that they want, and to a lesser extent many were influenced by the prospect of unemployment. We have already explored some of the subtleties of these issues for those wishing to enter work directly and those wishing to proceed to higher education. We now turn to the group as a whole.

The majority of young people from all groups regarded their future job prospects as a prime motive for continuing their education. Only five out of 211 respondents claimed that this was not even partly a reason, while over 80% gave an unequivocal 'yes' to the question. It seems again that these young people do believe that passing examinations will improve their job prospects.

The second most popular reason for continuing education was that students wished to enter another institution of further or higher education at a later date. Half of the respondents ticked 'yes' to this suggestion. The remaining options were less frequently chosen; only one in five students said they were continuing because their parents wanted them to, or because they liked studying, and one in seven because there were no jobs to go to. However, this last question received a relatively higher proportion of 'partly' responses: indeed, half the students thought that this was either a reason or partly a reason for their remaining in education. There was a slight suggestion that this was a more frequent reaction among the students at colleges.

There was a very slight tendency for white and Afro-Caribbean students at college to be more inclined to continue their education in the future. More marked was the difference in attribution of their parents' encouragement as a reason for attendance between students of South Asian ethnic origin and others. The former group, especially sixth-formers, were particularly likely to assign their parents a key role in the decision. These sixth-formers were more likely than their white counterparts to be aspiring to higher education.

Further education: entry and evaluations

When specific reasons for going to college are examined in contrast to overall reasons for continuing education, a slightly different picture emerges. The underlying aims of achieving qualifications and perhaps entering higher education remain vital, but in the particular choice of college rather than school social reasons are also very important.

We asked college students what they had to do to get their college place. Responses here appear in Table 13.

Table 13: FE students: to get college place (%)

	Asian	Afro-Caribbean	White
had interview	68.6	85.7	85.7
took written test	13.3	57.1	42.9
passed specified exam grades	56.3	71.4	28.6

There is a very slight suggestion that Afro-Caribbean students' entrance to college is or is perceived to be a more stringent experience than for other groups.

The seven Afro-Caribbean students applied for proportionately more courses and were rejected from more courses than other students. Whether or not their experience is generalisable, for the individuals concerned there was certainly a difference, with 71.4% of Afro-Caribbean further education students having made applications to other colleges and 42% having been rejected. Only 23.1% of white students had made such applications and only 15.4% had been rejected.

The hypothesis that Afro-Caribbean young people might find it more difficult to gain access to college is also supported modestly by an analysis of sixth-form students. As one of the potential reasons for entering continuing education, we asked sixth-formers if they had decided to stay on at school because they 'could not get on to a college course'. Five Afro-Caribbean respondents agreed, and only three each of pupils of white and South Asian ethnic origin. The responses, therefore, revealed only a 'slight tendency' for Afro-Caribbeans to find it more difficult to gain access to colleges.

Level of courses

It is notable that 34 sixth-formers, almost one in five of these respondents, were taking courses leading to their re-sitting the Certificate of Secondary Education. Even more intended to re-sit examinations for the General Certificate of Education. Sixty young people, over a quarter of those in continuing education, were intending to re-sit 'O' levels.

Overall there were no significant sex differences in the types of examination course undertaken. However, some differences did appear between and within ethnic groups. We shall look first at sixth forms. Afro-Caribbean students were more likely to be undertaking lower level courses than the remainder of young people at school. A greater proportion were re-sitting CSEs and taking Certificate of Extended Education courses and vocational subjects, while fewer were working for one or more 'A' levels. For 'A' levels this difference is highly significant for boys alone, as only two of the 21 Afro-Caribbean boys were taking an 'A' level course in the lower sixth, compared to five of the eight girls. The significant differences between groups in vocational courses undertaken arise in part from the comparatively low number of white students utilising this provision in sixth forms. In addition, 11 sixth-formers were working towards examinations validated by the Royal Society of Arts, seven for 'O'/'A' levels and 11 for other categories of examinations. The distributions of these types of courses do not noticeably affect the overall distribution of levels of examination between groups.

Given the low numbers of FE students, it is difficult to draw anything but the most tentative conclusions. However, it seems that white students tend to be more likely to follow the traditional pattern of utilising FE for 'vocational' courses and school for 'academic' subjects in the post-16 phase. Black young people, and particularly those with Afro-Caribbean backgrounds, seem more likely to take vocational courses in schools, and also to use colleges to take 'O' and 'A' levels.

Black students especially were likely to envisage taking 'A' levels in the equivalent of the third year sixth or later, while we also believe that some were hoping to do one-year 'A' level courses in college between 1983 and 1984.

Despite the longer-term 'A' level ambitions of black students, they appear to have been more frequently placed on 'vocational' courses involving work experience in both schools and colleges. Corresponding with their placement in vocational study, Afro-Caribbean students were significantly more likely than others to be undertaking link courses with local colleges. Nearly one in three claimed to 'go to a college course during school hours'. Only about 5% of others came in the same category.

Summary

This chapter reviews the enthusiasm of black young people to continue their education — particularly the enthusiasm of all Asians and Afro-Caribbean girls. Yet this enthusiasm is also associated with a lack of confidence and uncertainty of their own potential — a markedly greater uncertainty than whites. The preference to 'stay on', even though expressed as a means of enhancing employment characteristics, may for some also be a means of avoiding exposure to failure in the labour market.

Colleges of further education were favoured by a majority of young blacks either directly or after further time at school to build up stocks of 'O' levels or CSEs. Examination success rates for blacks in colleges of further education were far less skewed against them than in schools, but this may result from differential recruitment patterns rather than institutional factors. It was particularly interesting to notice that blacks used further education for academic and vocational purposes and whites for predominantly vocational purposes. Yet as in school many blacks, especially Afro-Caribbeans, tended to have a greater experience of work and link schemes than whites. There was also some evidence of more stringent college entry standards for Afro-Caribbeans, and for black students generally to have to find out about further education through informal rather than formal channels.

9. Young people in the labour market

Seeking employment

One hundred and twenty-five young people answered questionnaires intended for those in the cohort who had left full-time education. We consider their responses to work and unemployment in this chapter and their experiences in schemes for unemployed school leavers in the next. We emphasise that the numbers of respondents are small and may be unrepresentative, and that there are limits to generalising from our information. Table 14 illustrates the position of leavers in summer 1983 when the questionnaire was administered. Black young people, especially boys, are significantly less likely than whites to be in employment.

Table 14: Leavers: status at summer 1983

	Asian	Afro-Caribbean	White
BOYS			
in a full-time job	0	0	77.3%
unemployed/other	100%	100%	22.7%
GIRLS			
in a full-time job	66.7%	20.0%	72.1%
in a part-time job	11.1%	10.0%	9.3%
unemployed/other	22.2%	70.0%	18.6%

We have seen that white respondents were more likely to be employed at the time of the survey. They had also held more jobs since leaving school. These differences are exacerbated by the speed at which many of them found work. Almost half report finding a job within one month of leaving school, a position which only five blacks shared.

The unemployed

There were 36 respondents who classified themselves as 'not working'. The respondents comprise 18 boys and 18 girls. Of the boys, four are of Asian, seven of Afro-Caribbean and seven of white ethnic origins. The girls are divided rather differently — three, six and nine in each group respectively. Of these, 21 had never worked since leaving school and the majority of those who had never worked were black. In fact, all of the Asians and three-quarters of the Afro-Caribbeans had never had a job. Three-quarters of the unemployed respondents were registered as unemployed at their careers office or Jobcentre, and there was

45

little difference between ethnic groups in their propensity to register as unemployed.

Clearly black respondents are more worried about their plight in the job market. This may well be connected with the fact that most white young people had already demonstrated their capacity to get a job.

There was a suggestion from our survey that black unemployed retain greater faith in the efficacy of qualifications, though the inter-ethnic differences are not statistically significant. Neither are the differences in responses about the type of jobs sought, though there is apparently a tendency for black and especially Afro-Caribbean young people to be slightly more selective in their search strategies. This selectivity may also link with the prospective return to education of some of these respondents, and their greater participation in part-time education on their own account. It is, however, most unlikely that this can entirely explain their greater rate of unemployment.

Young workers

As we have seen, there were no black male respondents holding full-time paid jobs whatsoever, and only 14 black girls. There was no significant difference in the occupational levels of jobs actually achieved by girls of different ethnic groups, two-thirds of whom had entered various types of skilled non-manual occupations. The boys, however, were mainly in skilled or semi-skilled manual jobs.

White young people were disproportionately more likely to possess apprenticeships — because these were held by boys and no black boys held a full-time job. Apprentices tend to receive a more structured training than other young people, probably one leading to credentials, or at the least time-serving widely recognised as enhancing opportunities for jobs with alternative employers. However, we also asked 'Does your employer give you any training?'. This question did not produce significant differences between ethnic groups, with 57 of the 85 respondents answering 'yes'.

There were no significant differences in the take-home pay claimed by respondents of different ethnic groups, though girls of South Asian origin received rather less money (an average of £38.90 a week compared with £53.00 for Afro-Caribbeans and £50.60 for whites). The highest incomes claimed were £80 and £90, by a white boy and girl respectively. One question, which resulted in highly significant differences between groups, asked whether many of their close friends were unemployed. Only one black respondent answered 'no' to this question, compared to 39 whites.

Four out of every 10 young people in work actually found their jobs through family and friends, emphasising the importance of informal methods of recruitment at the present time. We have already noted that black parents of young people in our cohort were more likely to be unemployed, and that employed respondents claim that their close friends are more likely to be unemployed. Given the importance of family and friends for young people looking for work, these circumstances seem likely to enhance the disadvantages that black young people face in the employment market.

We have also noted that among our school leavers as a whole, black young people were significantly more likely to be unemployed. If leavers of all ethnic groups who had got jobs through their family are excluded from such a comparison, we find that black young people were even more likely to be unemployed. Only 11 out of 37 had full-time jobs, compared to 49 out of 68 whites. This difference is highly significant.

Unemployment and qualifications

We have seen that black young people who achieved some qualifications were more likely to stay on at school. How much might the relatively low qualifications of black leavers have affected their chances of getting a job? Among our respondents there seems to be a relationship between the level of examination results achieved and the likelihood of being unemployed. The numbers involved are small and the differences do not assume great significance, but the trend is clear. Those with 'O' levels or equivalent were more likely to be holding a full-time job, and less likely never to have had a job at all. However, at each level of examination results achieved, black respondents were far more likely to be unemployed than white.

Unemployment and parents' jobs

We have suggested that there may be a relationship between parents' occupational or employment statuses and the ability to implement the 'lads of dads' process in favour of their offspring and otherwise inform children of appropriate opportunities. Our evidence possibly detects signs of this among respondents, in addition to the processes we have already demonstrated. The evidence is slight, but certainly more respondents with employed fathers had held a full-time job since leaving school than those without. Young people with working mothers were also more likely to be in work themselves and to have held a job since leaving school.

Summary

Overall, our white respondents in the labour market were more likely to be employed and employed more frequently and rapidly than black. We have also shown that unemployment was partly related to family contacts, qualifications and the employment status of parents.

The experience of unemployment or even the likelihood of it reinforced the lack of confidence of black young people, making them more likely to wish they had decided to stay on in education — or had been allowed to do so. Black young people showed a higher incidence of part-time study, a higher rate of temporary jobs and fewer job applications. They cared more about being unemployed (especially Asians), especially when aware of white successes, and most were prepared to be geographically mobile. They had more unemployed friends. Yet, notwithstanding their situation in the labour market, they still tended to believe in the possibility of obtaining 'a good job' aided by education qualifications.

10. Schemes for unemployed school leavers

YOP schemes and young people in the labour market

A number of respondents offered opinions of Youth Opportunities schemes in response to our request for 'any more comments'. All opinions were critical, often echoing negative political appraisals with wide currency. We received no favourable comments.

Responses to our questionnaire illustrated the complexities of young people's attitudes to schemes. For some respondents, schemes can both be 'slave labour' and provide a useful training. This is, of course, not an illogical contradiction — there are situations in which both are true. That four-fifths of the respondents were prepared to say that schemes might be slave labour and more than four-fifths thought that they might provide useful training and might not be a waste of time, might well be valid, reflecting an awareness of the difficulties that young people face today. The caution exhibited in responses to the question as to whether schemes 'help you get jobs' might be similarly acute. Only 22% felt they would help, while 63.3% said 'perhaps' and 14.7% said 'no'. Research by the Manpower Services Commission and others has shown that some schemes may help, and others may not.

There are no statistically significant differences in responses to our suggested statements about YOP between those who have and have not been on schemes themselves — though there are slight tendencies which might have assumed significance with a larger sample. A higher percentage of YOP participants believed that schemes would not help them to get a job (20% as opposed to 10% of non-participants) but did give useful training (68% compared to 47%). Overall, it seems that the opinions, even of those on schemes, are not necessarily based on personal experience and may be pre-judged.

Among our respondents those known to have participated in YOP were significantly more likely to be unemployed. Black young people were also more likely to have participated in schemes. In the 12 months to July 1983, they had spent a mean of 4.1 months in schemes, the whites only two months.

Of the various types of YOP schemes on offer, other research suggests that those trainees undertaking WEEP courses are the most successful in moving on to real jobs after finishing their scheme. The figures provided by the area officer responsible for Bradford show that only one-third of black trainees were on WEEP schemes compared to nearly half the white trainees. However, only 50% of WEEP places were filled in Bradford throughout the period compared with 75-80% of non-WEEP places.

We cannot, however, provide any clear explanation for this. There may perhaps have been some element of preference amongst black young people for schemes which were clearly providing a 'course'. There were also some sponsors of community projects, a Community Relations Council-sponsored training workshop, and certain college courses under YOP regulations which might have been particularly likely to recruit black school leavers. One cannot therefore ascribe any imbalance purely to the placements advocated and managed by careers officers or to any antagonism exhibited by employers towards particular categories of young people.

Such disparity between black and white trainees may partially explain the lesser extent to which the former appear to find work after participating on schemes.

YTS and young people in continuing education

Our second set of questionnaires, administered at Easter 1983, coincided with the introduction of the Youth Training Scheme by the MSC. We therefore decided to ask members of the cohort still in full-time education about YTS. For many, it was a possible option for them to take at the end of their first year in the sixth form or at college. For the remainder, these questions could serve as an indicator of the effectiveness of dissemination of this new departure in training.

Although 80% of the young people claimed to have heard of YTS, they did not necessarily know much about the scheme. Little more than half knew that the allowance was to be £25 a week, and less than half that a scheme was intended to last one year. Afro-Caribbean students were rather better informed than the rest about both these points, with about 70% correct on each aspect. None of the inter-ethnic differences in this section assumes statistical significance at less than the 1% level, but in each case it is the Afro-Caribbean group that stands out as best informed. This is likely to be accounted for partly by these young people residing in areas where schemes have assumed a greater importance in the local youth economies, and perhaps by the slightly longer-term academic aspirations expressed by other groups.

Overall, the state of knowledge about YTS among those young people remaining in full-time education was perhaps less than satisfactory. Given the extent of national investment in the scheme, one might have hoped for more adequate dissemination at that crucial period. However, one must also hypothesise that opinions of YOP held by both teachers and pupils might have contributed to the comparative failure to communicate further details of its successor.

Schemes and ethnic minorities

MSC's statistics on take-up by ethnic group, with the exception of Bradford, were uneven at the time of our study. However, they suggest a tendency nationally for a lower percentage of black young people to be on Mode A schemes and consequently a higher percentage on Mode B, and within Mode B they are more likely to find themselves on B1 schemes offered by voluntary groups, training workshops and similar organisations under programmes arranged by MSC. This national perspective is confirmed by MSC local area tabulations, though each presents a slightly different picture of the distribution of young people on schemes by both mode and ethnic group.

We also found a tendency from the MSC data for ethnic minority trainees to be under-represented on WEEP, supporting also the 'interview survey'.

Conclusion

We would not wish to join the generally critical appraisal; indeed, the way in which the MSC has responded to its huge task is impressive and often remarkably successful. We are also conscious of the development of the Special Groups Division within MSC which has special responsibilities for the ethnic minority groups. As always, special provision denotes special treatment; as always this may or may not be beneficial to the recipients. Several commentators suggest that the effects are not beneficial for young blacks. In our view, it is too early to make a judgment.

We have reviewed the ambivalence of our respondents to MSC schemes – dislike of the work but an acceptance, sometimes grudging, of the potential for training and job-getting. Opinions seemed personal, not always to be based on first-hand experience – even by those who had received it – and may even be pre-judged.

There is a persistent pattern of lower black participation in WEEP and other schemes based on employers' premises which allow 'extended interviews'. Although it has been suggested that blacks are discriminated against in access to these schemes, our evidence in Bradford did not substantiate this. Our study of the availability of YTS information in schools confirmed the difficulty of effective delivery of careers information to young people in school.

11. Conclusions and recommendations

Conclusions

If there is a single theme that runs through this report it is the determination of very large numbers of young people from ethnic minority groups to persevere with their education in the hope of obtaining their desired occupations. This persistence is evident in many ways, in homework and extra schoolwork, investing time in school sixth forms, colleges of further education and part-time courses, and the keen desire to enter higher education.

This determination is frequently associated with occupational ambitions that are no higher than those of white pupils in the same schools and colleges. And even where these ambitions are higher, they are almost always appropriately linked to the qualifications which are being realistically pursued by the young people. It is this theme of persistence and willingness to invest both time and money for self-improvement which we wish to stress at the outset.

There are social processes in both schools and society at large that work to counteract the efforts of these young people. In schools, both at and below sixth form level, ethnic minority pupils may be placed on courses and entered for examinations at levels below those appropriate for their abilities and ambitions. Teachers may be unwilling to accept the existence of these processes, or even to redress them where they are aware of them. And when schools fail then young black people can find it difficult to enter colleges of further education.

In society at large, the effects of racial discrimination upon employment prospects appear to be severe. Even when young black people do attain appropriate qualifications, they do not obtain jobs in equal proportions to whites either before or after participating in schemes. We cannot report the experiences of young people in this situation extensively: only small numbers in our cohort had left education. However, we have outlined the incidence of unemployment amongst young black people using both local and national data.

Recommendations

We now offer a series of recommendations, all of which are based upon the evidence presented in our report. But even as we write labour market conditions continue to change; this final section of the report itself was completed in a month when the overall numbers of unemployed people reached a higher level than at any time before. These and a wide range of other changes must inevitably affect the context in which these recommendations are written.

Schools

- Black pupils give the schools a major vote of confidence by staying on in very large numbers. They do so for reasons arising from keen occupational aspirations (seldom unrealistic) which may be mixed with fundamental doubts about their capability and a desire not to expose themselves to failure in the labour market. We *recommend* that all schools take more active steps to justify and reward this high rate of staying on. In particular, we *recommend* very careful planning to be undertaken of the curriculum and organisation for the 16+ that takes full account of their ambitions, motivations and their uncertainties. Something more imaginative than a programme of CSE/'O' level re-sits may not only be desirable but also possible in most schools. A programme of pre-'A' level courses, vocationally-oriented 'O' level courses and some components of the new spectrum of technical and vocational school-leaving examinations being developed within the context of the Technical and Vocational Educational Initiative (TVEI) may offer a more attractive set of options. In addition to the examination work, a programme of non-examination activities that explore vocational, community and recreational opportunities could be devised, in consultation with the students, to help them to maximise their own resources and those of the neighbourhood.

- We *recommend* that the schools *should* pay particular attention to their procedures of allocation to sets, streams, bands and other work and ability groups so that they fully recognise not only the existing achievement but also the potential of their students. There is evidence in our report to indicate that this is by no means always done. Although labelling theory is fallible, it still offers a valuable explanation of much of the profile of expectations that surround children and teachers. Faulty allocation can lead to faulty achievement and it seems to be Afro-Caribbean children who suffer most severely in this process.

- We *recommend* that schools should carefully examine their procedures for examination entries and allocation to examination groups to ensure fair treatment of all racial groups and also to ensure that individual pupils are given the fullest opportunity to attain the highest level qualification they are capable of.

- We *recommend* that schools make particular efforts in their curriculum arrangements to ensure that they are offering all children the best chance to identify and develop the most marketable skills that are appropriate to their chances in the labour market. We *recommend* that schools seek to identify and help to develop the capacities of their minority group pupils. It may be that more schools could allow their pupils to return after an unsatisfactory trial of the labour market. We recognise in making this recommendation that there is a thin dividing line between emphasising strengths and building upon them and identifying differences and stereotyping them. With equal conviction, we *recommend* schools not to 'ghettoise' their ethnic minority pupils by providing them with a 'soft option' curriculum in which they can succeed. Such an attempt can do no more than substitute low attainment in mainstream marketable skills with high attainment in non-marketable skills. We *recommend* schools to deliver a curriculum that is relevant to the potentials of black and white children and which recognises their full range of capabilities.

- We *recommend* schools to pay careful attention to the quality control of the experience of their black students. On some occasions we found it difficult to obtain a clear picture of the participation in the curriculum, of the results of tests and written assignments. We are convinced that the best interests of all children are served by careful recording of achievement which can be used for enhanced diagnosis and guidance and the identification of potential.
- Whatever the cause when black children behave badly, formal punishment can often reinforce negative racial stereotypes and hence lower the expectations of achievement of black pupils. This is particularly the case if they are seen as involving unequal treatment. We *recommend* schools to take particular care in their strategies of punishing black pupils. This applies not only to 'in school' punishments such as withdrawal of status but also to exclusion and withdrawal of support for employment or continuing education.
- We *recommend* all schools to reinforce their efforts to inform and involve all parents in their children's education.
- In most British universities and polytechnics, overseas students with modest commands of English regularly obtain Masters and PhD degrees. Such students with only a relatively modest initial language capacity find that their fluency increases most effectively as they work in their chosen subject. We *recommend* schools to consider similar approaches with ethnic minority children.
- We *recommend* that all schools developing the TVEI should pay particular attention to the ways in which black children may benefit. It could well be that these could provide more marketable attainments than the CSE or CEE courses undertaken by some sixth form and college pupils.
- We *recommend* that schools offering work experience programmes pay particular attention to familiarising employers and potential employers with the full potential and capabilities of black children and that all other contacts of the school be also used for this purpose.
- We *recommend* schools to take anti-racist guidelines seriously. In some schools there may still be genuinely racist teachers. We *recommend* that such teachers should be given a clear opportunity to consider whether or not they are still suitable to be members of the profession. All this is not to say that the schools must become obsessionally sensitive. If teachers and pupils are aware of the issues, they will be able to handle the prejudice that frequently occurs in the playground, the community and the workplace in a way that helps both black and white children to be unharmed by it and, ultimately, to diminish it.
- We *recommend* that all teachers recognise that there are many ways in which their responsibility for the guidance and encouragement and support may be shown. Furthermore, the way in which 'diagnostic' guidance is offered needs to be especially sensitive so that correct guidance may not be ignored for incorrect reasons.
- We would urge the fundamental truth that schools and their teachers must start with the child where he or she is. To paraphrase the precept of Bernstein, 'if the consciousness of the teacher is to be in the mind of the child then first of all the consciousness of the child must be in the mind of the teacher'.

Further education

- We *recommend* that further education establishments present the opportunities they offer more clearly and directly to black and white young people. There seems a need for access provision to bridge the gap between low or non-existent school attainment and further education. At the moment this gap tends to be bridged by a further year of re-sits in the schools. We *recommend* that further education establishments take the initiative to develop such courses in liaison with the schools.

- We *recommend* that further education institutions should emphasise that they are not only a second-chance institution where an alternative venue is offered to take 'O' and 'A' levels and similar 'in-school' qualifications, but rather that they are first-chance institutions for those for whom school may have been irrelevant or an experience of failure.

- We *recommend* colleges of further education to be alert to the full potential of their black students. This recommendation is reinforced by the suggestion of higher thresholds of admission for young black students in some colleges of further education.

Careers service

- We *recommend* that all careers services be required to adopt clear and uniform statistical procedures to ensure a true local and national data base.

- There was lack of evidence of clear monitoring to identify the instance of 'missing persons' particularly of black young people who left school, had obtained neither work nor YOP entry, or registered as unemployed (25%). (This problem is not, of course, confined to black young people.) We *recommend* that the careers service persevere in its attempts to ensure complete coverage in the interests of the young and of society at large. Our other recommendations are designed to reinforce this central need.

- We *recommend* that the careers service gives considerably more attention to the ways in which young people are prepared for interviews, perhaps by finding ways in which young people can learn about the world of work before their interview.

- We *recommend* that the careers service starts its sequence of interviewing for some young people ahead of the time now currently used for most school leavers in order to assure equality of opportunity in applications for all categories of employment available for school leavers.

- We *recommend* that the careers service refines its procedures for not only recognising but also acting upon evidence of discrimination. We also *recommend* that the service institutes more effective procedures for monitoring referrals to training schemes and employment interviews, to assist young black people to receive equal opportunities to acquire both marketable skills and paid employment. Associated with this, we *recommend* a considerable extension in the arrangements for in-service training within the careers service in which appropriate aspects of race awareness training play a proper part.

- We *recommend* that the careers service literature made available by the careers service is not only comprehensive and readily available to all young people, but also that it is carefully scrutinised to avoid presenting stereotypes of racial differentiation in employment.

Local education authorities

Our main recommendation to LEAs is that they seek to implement our previous recommendations to their schools and colleges. In addition we offer the following:

- We *recommend* that all authorities develop guidelines for their institutions and staffs so that they may help to eliminate discriminatory, prejudicial and racist behaviour.
- We *recommend* that all local education authorities develop strategies to identify materials in the schools which carry discriminatory messages and, in particular, that literature which indicates differentiated occupation roles between black and white people should not be available to influence occupational decisions by black or white young people.
- We *recommend* that local education authorities recognise the gulf that exists between many low achieving young people in the schools and their aspirations for entry to further education. This gulf is not always unbridgeable and we *recommend* that all local authorities seek to develop a range of access routes for entry to their further education establishments.
- We *recommend* that all local authorities take steps to ensure that their whole advisory service (and not just those members specifically concerned with multi-ethnic education) are fully aware of what is needed and seek to implement changes. This could include the development of relevant in-service courses, guidance and counselling to individual teachers and to school staffs as a whole, and an alert presence in the schools.
- We *recommend* that all local authorities take urgent steps to explore the workings of local careers services, to ensure an effective delivery to all young people.

Department of Education and Science

- We *recommend* the department use the School Examinations Council to bear in mind the position of candidates from ethnic minorities in renewing criteria for examinations at 16+.
- Not all schools provide a curriculum for all their pupils that is effectively directed to identifying and developing their marketing skills. We *recommend* that the new Curriculum Council be urged to pay particular attention to this aspect of curriculum.
- There is an urgent need for fuller information on the activities of the 18-19-year-old population. For the most part these young people have completed schooling, further education or participation in MSC schemes. We *recommend* that the department, in liaison with other relevant ministries, seek ways of rectifying this information gap.

- There is a need for a concerted programme of in-service training for teachers and careers officers concerned with the placement and guidance of young people from the ethnic minority groups. Wherever possible, it is desirable that employers participate in such training. It is *recommended* that pre-vocational programmes be augmented to pay particular attention to this need.
- Not all schools have considered thoroughly the opportunities presented to them by young black students who present themselves for continuing education in the schools after the minimum leaving age. We *recommend* that the DES and HMI give urgent attention to ways in which schools may be helped to develop appropriate provision.
- We *recommend* that continuing pressure be placed on teacher training establishments to ensure that all students develop an appropriate sensitivity and perceptiveness for working with minority group adolescents.
- More generally, we *recommend* that all published reports by DES and HMI, ranging from those on individual schools through to major reports on curriculum and organisation, should be written with an awareness of the special problems to which we have drawn attention and, where appropriate, specific mention of alleviatory strategies should be offered.

The Manpower Services Commission

- We *recommend* that ethnic monitoring should be given a very high priority by the MSC and should include evaluation of the participation in, and employment outcomes resulting from, schemes. This should pay particular attention to the level of black participation in schemes based on employers' premises and others which give opportunity to experience 'extended interviews' with potential employers. We also *recommend* that particular care should be taken to ensure that racial discrimination, both overt and covert, is not practised by colleges, managing agents or by employers utilised for placements. We *recommend* that agents and employers receive advice from the Commission for Racial Equality to ensure that discrimination does not occur.
- We *recommend* that the MSC and its officers should take particular care to dissociate the notion of special needs from that of racial disadvantage. This becomes especially important with the establishment of the Special Groups Division with its concern for minority groups.
- We *recommend* that area offices of the MSC undertake monitoring of publicity and recruitment procedures and their results.
- We *recommend* that MSC pay particular attention to the incidence and performance of young black people in its TVEI in the schools.

Some of the changes we suggest involve additional costs and resources. We hope that they are seen to be of sufficient importance to be justified even in present economic conditions. But most involve changes of perception and attitude on the part of individuals and require no new money. Moreover, such changes, by enhancing human capability and diminishing the waste of human resources, may give rise to substantial economic gain.

It has often been said that schools and colleges cannot fundamentally change the labour market; they cannot eradicate structural unemployment. But there is some limited evidence, confirmed in our report, that schools can enhance the employability of their young people and that this may have a small but beneficial effect on the labour market. Some schools might even develop entrepreneurial characteristics in their young people which can lead them to create their own employment opportunities. But of even greater importance is the achievement of a number of schools in helping to create a more just and equitable distribution of opportunities in our society. We believe that our recommendations can facilitate this process that leads to greater justice between the races and, in so doing, makes a contribution to the diminution of racial tension and bitterness.

Other publications of interest

Advisory Approaches to Multicultural Education
Arnold Mathews
Surveys the organisational framework and policies of local advisors
£1.50

Racism and Discrimination in Britain: a select bibliography 1970-83
Paul Gordon and Francesca Klug
£3.50

Different Worlds: racism and discrimination in Britain
Paul Gordon and Francesca Klug
An illustrated pamphlet suitable for use in secondary schools
£1.00 (revised edition forthcoming)

Race and Immigration: the Runnymede Trust bulletin
Monthly bulletin covering all aspects of race relations and immigration in Britain
£12 pa (institutions), £10 pa (voluntary bodies), £8 pa (individuals)

Other Research Reports

'Education For All': a summary of the Swann report
50p

The Chinese Community in Britain: the Home Affairs Committee report in context
£1.25

Employment, unemployment and black people
£1.50

Racial violence and harassment
£1.50

Available from the Runnymede Trust, 178 North Gower Street, London NW1 2NB

Please add 15% for p&p (minimum 25p)